THE ART OF COMMUNICATION

THE ART OF COMMUNICATION

By
Kailash Chandra Verma

KALPAZ

First Published 2013

Published by

Kalpaz Publications
C-30, Satyawati Nagar,
Delhi-110052
Ph. : 9212142040
E-mail: kalpaz@hotmail.com

Laser Typesetting : Rudra Computer Graphics, Delhi
Printed at : G. Print Process, Delhi

Cataloging in Publication Data—DK
Courtesy: D.K. Agencies (P) Ltd. <docinfo@dkagencies.com>

Verma, Kailash Chandra.
The Art of Communication / Kailash Chandra Verma.
p. cm.
Includes bibliographical references (p.) and index.

ISBN 9788178359823 (HB)

1. Communication. 2. Oral communication. 3. Language arts. I. Title.

DDC 302.23 23

Dedicated to

My Wife INDIRA

&

Lucky Trio

Manish, Rishi, Rajnish

Contents

Acknowledgements

I am thankful to all my friends and readers for encouraging me to bring out and complete the task of second edition. I also wish to thank them for their constant encouragement. I also wish to thank all those who gave me valuable comments on manuscript and suggestions for some excellent re-orientation especially to Mr. B. K. Saxena and Mr. P.K. Shrivastava for their valuable contribution. I thank finally to my wife Indira who not only provided the encouragement and supported to complete the task but also read the draft with unfailing eyes and to my son Manish, Rishi, Rajnish and their wives Monica, Ruchi and Shilpi and my naughty grand son Pratyush for their active participation in discussion to steer me in the right direction.

Preface

Communication is a global phenomenon that binds the people in a family, society, and organisation throughout the world. It is an art. Whether it is a family, society or organisation communication takes place in every walk of human life. A newly born baby too sense non-verbal ques with the mother for all its needs. The mother interprets, understands and responds to the ques – communication occurred.

Expression is a part of human nature, they communicate to express verbally or non-verbally through words, body-face, eye, gesture, posture, appearance etc. Message can be sent in number of ways. It requires effective communication skills in both sending and receiving the message for its appropriate response.

Nobody listens everybody but somebody listens anybody to improve upon his or her skills to communicate.

The success of managers, leaders, administrators, teachers, trainers and interviewee depends upon their ability to communicate effectively.

The roles, the managers of organisations play are heavily geared to the need to be an effective communicator. These managers tend to spend upon 80 per centd of their time in communicating. An overwhelming proportion of their time is spent in generating information.

The process of communication is thus of utmost importance to everyone as it enables to carryout day to day functions and responsibilities. To succeed, one has to develop effective relevant communication skill.

An attempt has been made in this package to synthesise and orient the available information about communication and add some more areas that are often overlooked. After reading this one may have clear picture and better understanding of communication, interpersonal communication, organisational communication, communication modes, the process, the problem and diagnostic steps to overcome deficiencies and fill the gap and the ways to improve effectiveness as communicator.

Kailash Chandra Verma
• 755 - 2495618

1

Introduction

Communication is considered to be the most important and most effective ingredient of the management process. Interpersonal communication is fundamental to all managerial activities. All other functions involve some form of directions and feedback. Effective management is a function of effective communication. Many operations have failed because of poor communication, misunderstood messages and unclear instructions. Even in life, in general, communication plays a very important role among friends, within the family and in all social circles. "Failure to communicate" is many times the cause for lost friendships, divorces and distances between parents and children. "My father does not understand me" is the common cry of a teenager. Accordingly, communication plays an important role in all walks of human life as well as organisational life.

Communication is defined as "the process of passing information and understanding from one person to another". It means transmitting and sharing of ideas, opinions, facts and information in a manner that is perceived and understood by the receiver of the communication. It is a meaningful interaction among people where the thoughts are transferred from one person to another in a manner such that the meaning and value of such thoughts is same in the minds of both the sender as well as the receiver of the communication.

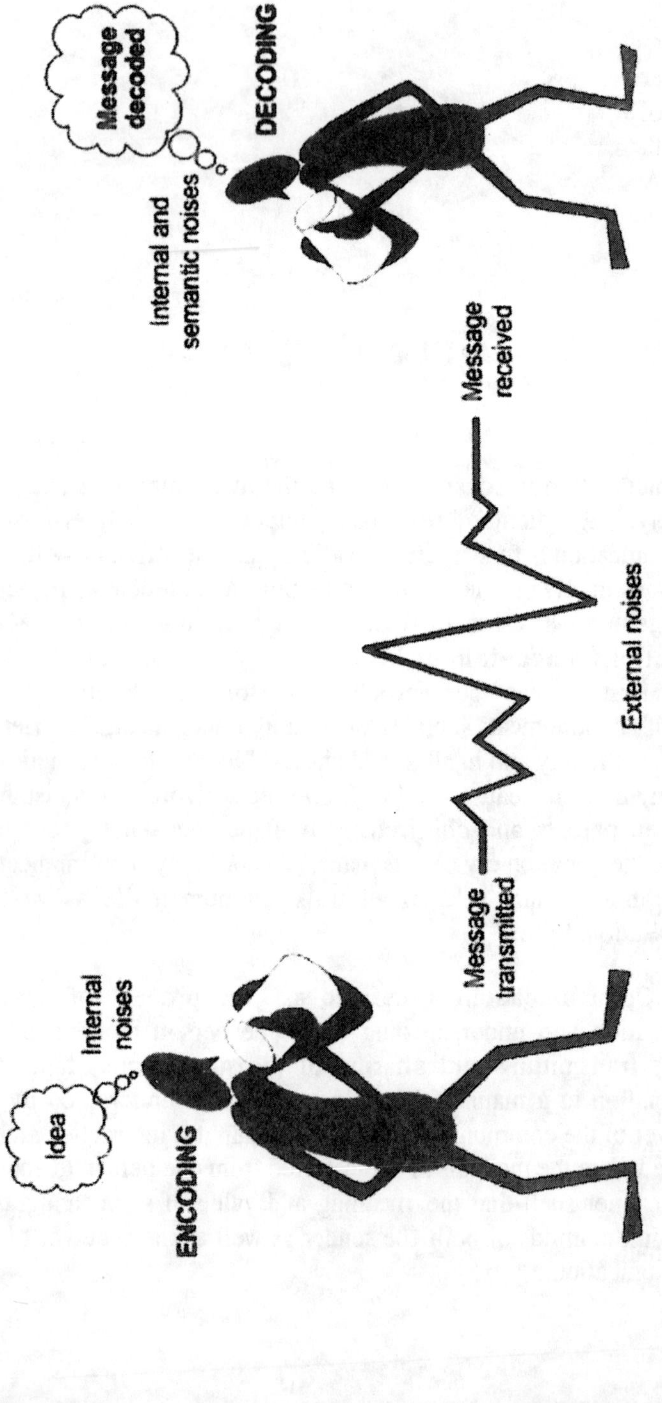
Idea
Internal noises
ENCODING
Message transmitted
External noises
Message received
Internal and semantic noises
Message decoded
DECODING

Fig. 1.1.

Effective communication is very essential for management to successfully perform its functions. It is an essential ingredient in management-employee relations. Most of the conflicts in business are not basic but are caused by misunderstood motives and ignorance of facts. Proper communications between interested parties reduce the points of friction and minimise those that inevitably arises. Accordingly, by proper communication and sharing of information, the management takes the employees in to confidence and make them more knowledgeable about problems and policies of the enterprise. The scope for a two-way means of consulting and exchanging facts, opinions and ideas between management and employees pertain to:

- Knowledge of policies and objectives of an enterprise.
- Knowledge of results and achievements from these policies.
- Knowledge of plans and prospects for the future.
- Knowledge of conditions of service.
- Knowledge of ways and means of improving efficiency and productivity.
- Knowledge of all aspects of industrial safety, health and welfare.

Information and knowledge about all these aspects makes the operations of the organization comparatively trouble free and it is the management's responsibility to ensure that employees have obtained all the necessary feedback relative to it. According to Peter Drucker, a manager does not handle people; he motivates, guides and organizes people to accomplish their goals. His effectiveness depends upon his ability to communicate well with the employees. Good communication is the foundation of sound management. It is through communication that workers become aware of their own duties and responsibilities as well as the instructions and orders from the upper levels of management hierarchy and also their own suggestions, grievances and feedback. Proper communication eliminates delays, misunderstanding, confusion, distortions and bottlenecks and improves coordination and control. It improves productivity by developing and maintaining good human relations in the organisation. It is a basic tool for motivation and improved morale. Supervision and leadership are impossible without it.

Communication is a dynamic force in shaping the organisational behaviour. Communication is considered as one of the three important elements of an organisation along with common purpose and willingness to serve. Communication may also be linked with concept of authority. The authority flows down through the channels of communications. The authority can lose its meaning if the channels of communications are blocked or if the communication is misunderstood or if the strength of communication is diluted.

Following are the seven communications factors in an organisation, which are a function of objective authority:

1. The channel of communication must be clearly set and be known to all.

2. Some channel of communication should reach every member of the organisation.

3. The line of communication should be as direct as possible.

4. There should be no blockage in the line of communication and the complete formal line should be used.

5. The communicator should be highly skilled in the art of communication.

6. The line of communication should be constantly kept open.

7. Every communication should be authenticated.

Organisations would be OK if it wasn't for the people who work in them, complained a frustrated consultant after an unsuccessful presentation of a communications improvement proposal to a board of directors. They don't listen, they don't try to, understand. How much his reaction was due to his own inability to communicate effectively or the uselessness of his proposal is unknown, but ask any manager what one of his major problems in any organisation is and he will reply 'Communications'!

What is so important about communication that managers and employees get so frustrated and uptight about it? Why do we need effective communication in an organisation? At a personal level, why do you need to be an effective communicator?

Developing communications skills is like learning to play contract bridge. You need to learn the rules and the conventions. You also need a partner to practice with and you need to learn how well you are doing, so that you can improve on your areas of weakness in bidding or playing. And it is only with practice and feedback that you will develop into a good bridge player or an effective communicator.

1.1 What is Communication?

Communication can be considered as a personal process that involves the transfer of information and also involves some behavioural input. Communication is something people do. It does not exist without people taking some form of action. It has all to do with relationships between people. It can be very complex or very simple; very formal or informal - all depends on the nature of the message to be passed, and on the relationship between the sender and the receiver.

It consists of the transfer of information and understanding between parts and people in an organisation, and the various modes and media involved in communication interchanges. Effective communication therefore is critical to the success of an organisation.

Look at the changes that are occurring in organizations today:

- They are becoming more complex, both in structure and technology.
- Economic and market conditions are forcing greater efficiency and quality in manufacturing and services.

- Government legislation requires managers to interpret the changing implications for policies and practices in their own organisation.

- People at work, especially the younger ones, are expecting more from their employers - not just higher wages, but also greater personal and job satisfaction.

- They are becoming more dependent on horizontal communication channels. With increased complexity, information needs to flow quickly between specialists rather than go up and back down the hierarchy, with its inevitable delay and message distortion.

So when we look at the changes that are taking place in organisations today, it is clear that managers, to be effective, require communication performance at hitherto unheard of levels of excellence.

Some of the common answers to the question why to communicate? Are as follows:

- It leads to greater effectiveness.

- It keeps people in the picture.

- It gets people involved with the organisation and : Increases motivation to perform well.

- Increases commitment to the organisation.

- It makes for better relationships and understanding between: Supervisor, Subordinates and Colleagues; People within the organisation and outside it.

- It helps people to understand the need for change; How they should manage it; How to reduce resistance to change.

- There also needs to be a clear message, which must be understood by the recipient.

- Communication permeates every aspect of management. In fact, it is inherent in every process where human beings interact. It is a process that goes on, on its own - irrespective of whether you will it or not.

- No amount of resources, plans of actions or efforts can be made dynamic without the alchemy of communication.

- However, proper communication, that is, a message reaching its target without distortion and evoking the desired reaction, is not easy. It is very delicately balanced on numerous equally delicately balanced factors. Most of these factors are related to the imponderables of human behaviour and psychology. The challenge to you as a communicator lies in your adopting within your ongoing management style an integrated synthesis of these delicately - balanced factors.

- Communication is not just a question of ensuring that your information or instructions are conveyed up or down the line in precise terms. It has very much to do with feelings and ideas, with morale and motivation - on both sides. It is certainly not merely a matter of your perfecting only the techniques by which messages can be put across.

- In order for communication to play its real role of ensuring understanding and motivation among people for contributing their best, it is essential that all facets of an organisation are based on clear, and clearly-spelt out, objectives and on sincerity of purpose. It also requires mutual trust. There must exist an innate faith in the trustworthiness of the superiors in the organisation.

- For this, it is neither necessary nor possible that a honeymoon relationship must exist among people at various levels. In fact, you could be tough negotiators, hard taskmasters, and you may sometimes have to engage yourself in trails of strength. AH that can be understandable and acceptable - and can even be conducive to effective communication - as long as there is mutual trust between you and your people about the intentions and integrity on both sides.

It follows naturally that, after all the song and dance about perfection in the tools and techniques of communication, the credibility of the communicator as perceived by the communicatee is the very essence of communication.

1.2 The Art of Communication

Communication is one of the corner stones of the relationships. The way in which we talk to one another often determines how successful our relationships will be. This can be especially true with regards to the communication that occurs between parent and child.

Try to communicate with one another and ways to improve communication skills. So, what is communication really? The Merriam – Webster dictionary defines communication as a process by which information is exchanged between individuals through a common system of symbols, signs or behaviour. In other words the way we exchange information's with another.

Communication can be broken into two main types: (i) Verbal (ii) Non-verbal. Verbal communication requires the spoken

Fig. 1.2. Dance the Unique Form of Communication.

words (obviously) where as non-verbal communication involves gestures, facial expressions and postures.

1.3 Dance – The Unique Form of Communication

Dance was the first form of communication. There are so many similarities that it is hard to disagree. Dance involves patterns, movement, and creativity. Participants as well as observers can enjoy it.

There are as many styles as people. Tastes vary. Standards differ. Styles change. Trends come and go. But dance has been and will always be part of the human community. Once a dance is performed it can never be recaptured in the same way again; it is unrepeatable and irreversible. Even the simplest of dances involves thousands of intricate and complex manoeuvres. It may well be one of the highest and most unique forms of human expression. So, too,

Fig. 1.3. Dance Involves Patterns Movement and Creativity.

is communication. The list of similarities could be quite lengthy indeed. A few of the more important ones are highlighted below.

1.3.1 Communication is Used for Multiple Purposes

People dance for a variety of reasons: to entertain, to inform, to persuade, to insight, and even to seduce. Some dance for themselves - a form of self-expression - while some dance for others. The same can be said of communication.

Communication effectiveness cannot be limited to either the "results" or "understanding" criteria. Effectiveness only can be determined in light of the communicator's goals - Whatever they may be - including obfuscation, confusion or deception. Whether these are legitimate goals is an ethical question, just as there will always be questionable forms of dancing. Hence, there is no single measure of communication effectiveness, just as there is no one criterion to evaluate all dances.

1.3.2 Communication Involves the Coordination of Meanings

Dancers have to learn to coordinate their movements with one another regardless of the type of music. They must learn how to move together even though they do not necessarily share one another's reality. That is, dance partners see the situation differently but they know their appropriate roles and responses communicators do, as well, it is not always necessary or even desirable to totally share meaning to communicate, as long as participants know how to respond in their roles or according to the "rules of the game".

Communication is the process by which persons correlate, maintain and alter patterns of social order, but... the coordination of talk through which patterns of order emerge is not necessarily based on mutual understanding or a shared social reality.

That in order to understand the communication process, there is a need to look beyond the interpretations of messages how messages facilitate social order, maintain structure, and set up patterns is of prime importance. How does communication help or hinder the process of coordination's in an organisation? Couples who dance are evaluated, in part, on the degree to which their actions are coordinated with one another. The evaluation of communication effectiveness is judged similarly. Clumsiness, whether self inflicted or induced by others, is not rewarded in organisations or dance studios.

1.3.3 Communication Involves Co-orientation

In order to coordinate actions, dancers must learn to co-orient. They must be able to sense one another's cues, anticipate their partner's possible actions, and know the appropriate responses. So, too, do communicators. When communication breaks down, it is not always the result of misunderstandings, but rather that people have failed to co-orient; they have no adequate predictive capacity. Effective communicators are able to forecast with some accuracy the actions of others, their responses, and interpretations.

The seeming ease with which professional dancers whirl, pirouette, and leap in to one another's arms is deceptive. With long hours of practice, they can do this even when improvising because they are responding to one another's subtle cues. What is astonishing is that they can do all of this while both are constantly in motion. It is not like trying to get oriented while lost in a forest by calculating position in relation to some fixed object. Rather the "objects" both moving and they must simultaneously be orienting with one another. And this is precisely the complex and difficult challenge facing communicators who must simultaneously orient to each other while both are constantly changing.

How can dancers cope with the tremendous range of possible movements? How can all the possibilities be mastered? Communicators, like dancers, develop rules of thumb to cope with the uncertainties. In almost every style of dance there are rules of some sort, whether written or unwritten. Principles and rules should all be studied by aspiring dancers and choreographers if they are to create the style and qualities of movement necessary to communicate the mood, emotion, theme, and story of classical dance. Years of excellence are distilled in these rules, which, in turn, allow the dancers to co-orient.

Communicators, as well, develop a wide range of implicit rules that govern conversations. There are rules concerning who has the right to initiate or terminate a conversation, and what topics are appropriate to speak about and under what conditions. The list could go on, but the point is that the rules affect the conversation in much the same way that rules of dance constrain movement. Conversational rules, too, are a way to handle all the uncertainty and distil the essence of learning into a few easily manageable units. It is by enacting these rules that people coordinate their actions in the organisation.

To be an effective communicator, one must learn the special rules that apply in different settings. They, of course, vary from person to person, department to department and organisation to organisation. But that does not mean that a whole new set of rules needs to be learned when experiencing a new situation just as there are fundamental dance steps. But effective communicators also learn the special rules of each setting.

Rather, people are actively engaged in negotiating the rules, particularly during the first stages of relationships. This is why the orientation of new employees is so important.

1.3.4 Communicators Develop a Repertoire of Skills that may Pass from the Level of Consciousness

Beginning dancers have to consciously think about each movement in executing a pirouette. for instance. Over time they no longer think about how to execute each movement; they become concerned less with body mechanics and more with artistry. The apparent naturalness and ease of execution comes from years of practice, as movements that were once conscious now merge into the subconscious. Communicators learn in much the same way. When we learn a foreign language we have to think more consciously about syntax and semantics. But over time, through trial and error, we learn the rules and can speak with apparent ease.

When training employees to become better negotiators, existing set of rules needs to be refined. For example, it is important to know that concessions should be offered slowly, not all at once. At first, consciously trying to do this seems awkward, but with practice it becomes natural. The same kinds of procedures are effective in teaching, interviewing, public speaking, and motivation skills. And this precisely the technique used by dance instructors when they point out a motion that should be consciously attended to in order to execute a graceful manouvre.

1.3.5 Communication can be Viewed as a Patterned Activity

Choreographers map out patterns for their dances, a kind of circuit diagram drawn with arrows. Even with improvisational dances, a map can be drawn of the dancer's movement. Likewise, there are patterns of interaction in a conversation. The patterns are a by product of the rules of interaction used by the communicators. In other words, the patterns are the net result of the way the enacted rules interlock with one another. The interaction rules are viewed through a telescope lens, while the patterns are seen through a wide-angle lens.

Expert chess players who are familiar with an adversary's style of play (i.e., personal rules) frequently are able to sense deep but recurring patterns to their opponents games, not move by move but in a more general sense. Communicators, like amateur chess players, may not be aware of their own patterns but perceptive observers, kibitzers, can see them.

1.3.6 The Beauty of Communication is a Function of the Degree of Coordination

The aesthetic appreciation of the dance flow from the intricate patterns of coordination, the way in which it all fits together, so too, with communication. The greater the coordination between communicators, the more effective it is. They learn to anticipate one another's reactions and possible meanings. They are able to co-orient. They know the way in which the environment affects communication. This is what communicators aim for in organisations.

To be sure, there are some communication situations that require more specialised skills than others. Learning to negotiate effectively, for instance, requires more co-orientation than does giving a speech. Employees have different levels of skill. For some, communication is easy. But as with dancing, anyone can refine and improve his/her skills.

1.4 The Art of Good Communication

This goal is not very difficult to achieve, all that is required is to be geared up with the correct skills, style and ammunition. Here are some tips that will help you in making positive impressions with others and enhance your success.

Be Confident

The first important skill is to be confident and to have the skill of being able to gel in any environment, company and occasion.

Practice Good Listening Skills

The next important feature is to be a good listener. You can never be able to communicate and converse with someone if you don't listen to what that person says. You will get a chance to put in your views but before that be patient and listen to what the other person has to say.

Think Before You Speak

Always think before you speak. Take time to put your thoughts together rather than blurt something out that you will have to repent saying.

Be Updated

Be aware of the world around you and keep your current events updated so as to be able to participate in intellectual conversations and this way you will be able to communicate with more people.

Don't Pretend

Don't pretend that you know everything and nod your head to everything that the other person is saying. There is no harm or shame in acknowledging that you are not aware of that topic and in fact you can get to learn something new.

Stay Away from Gossip

Stay away from gossiping and also indulge in intelligent and healthy conversation.

Always avoid sensitive topics, especially when you don't know the people very well around you, like religion, politics and personal life. You don't want to get caught up in arguments and fights.

When someone starts talking about his or her problems be a good listener but don't offer advice. If someone does ask for your advice, sharing a similar experience you've had but don't sit into the advisory chair.

In conclusion the most important thing is - be yourself.

1.5 Effectiveness

Nowhere is this orientation more evident than when managers are asked about the meaning of effective communication. There are typical responses:

- "Being able to clearly and precisely put my thoughts into words."
- "Speaking with credibility and authority on topics I know about."
- "Getting the result I want by taking to my people."

Certainly managers should seek to speak clearly, concisely, and with credibility in order to achieve results. Yet, re-examination of each of those statements in light of the underlying assumptions is revealing as shown below. In short, the underlying premise is that managers are responsible for accurately encoding their thoughts into language; rather like selecting, aiming, and firing arrows at a

Communication Effectiveness	*Underlying Assumptions*
Being able to clearly and precisely put my thoughts into words	What is clear and precise to one person is clear and precise to another.
Speaking with credibility and authority.	Credibility is something the speaker possesses and not something given to the speaker by the audience.
Getting the result I want by talking to my people.	Communication is primarily a one-way activity.

target. Receivers of messages are viewed as passive information processors that react appropriately if the words are on the mark.

1.6 What is Effective Communication?

Communication is effective only when the people to whom you are communicating - receive your message, understand it, remember it, and - here's the clincher-respond to it appropriately. If your message doesn't succeed in these four areas, you're not communicating. This may be represented as follows :

Message

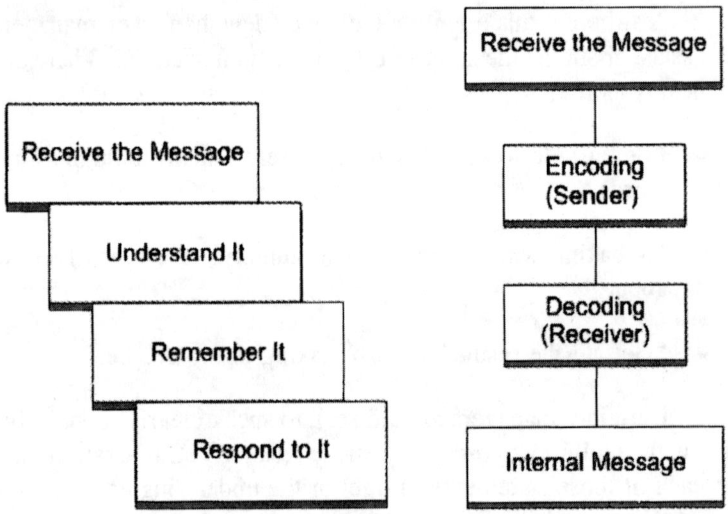

Fig. 1.4. Effective Communication.

A team that doesn't communicate effectively experiences division and lack of commitment. It wastes time and accomplishes little. Discussions drag on with little or no progress. However, a team that communicates well makes timely progress and achieves its goals.

1.7 The Importance of Communication

Effective communication is important for two reasons. First, communication is the process by which the management functions of planning, organising, leading and controlling are accomplished. Second, communication is the activity to which managers devote an overwhelming proportion of their time.

The process of communication makes it possible for managers to carry out their task responsibilities. Information must be communicated to managers so that they will have a basis for planning; the plans must be communicated to others to be carried out. Organising requires communicating with people about their job assignments. Leading requires managers to communicate with subordinates so that group goals can be achieved. Oral, written, and increasingly, electronic communications are an essential part of controlling. Managers can carry out their management functions only by interacting with and communicating with others. The communication process is thus the foundation for the management functions. A large share of managerial time is devoted to the activity of communication. Rarely are managers alone at their desks thinking, planning, or contemplating alternatives. In fact, managerial time is spent largely in face-to-face, electronic, or telephone communication with subordinates, peers, supervisors, suppliers or customers. When not conferring with others in person or on the telephone, managers may be writing or dictating memos, letters or reports - or perhaps reading memos, letters or reports sent to them. Even in those few periods when managers are alone, they are frequently interrupted by communications. For example, one study of middle and top managers found that they could work uninterruptedly for half an hour or more, only once every two days.

Henry Mintzberg, has described the manager's job in terms of three types of roles. Communication plays a vital part in each:

1. In their interpersonal roles, managers act as the figurehead and leader of their organisational unit, interacting with subordinates, customers, suppliers and peers in the organisation. Mintzberg cited studies indicating that managers spend about 45 per cent of their contact time with peers, about 45 per cent with people outside their units, and only about 10 per cent with superiors.

2. In their informational roles, managers seek information from peers, subordinates and other personal contacts about anything that may affect their job and responsibilities. They also disseminate interesting or important information in return.

In addition, they provide suppliers, peers and relevant groups outside the organisation with information about their unit as a whole.

3. In their decisional roles, managers implement new projects, handle disturbances and allocate resources to their unit's members and departments. Some of the decisions that manager's make will be reached in private, but they will be based on information that has been communicated to the managers. The managers, in turn, will have to communicate those decisions to others.

Thus, the communication is the foundation of management functions as shown below :

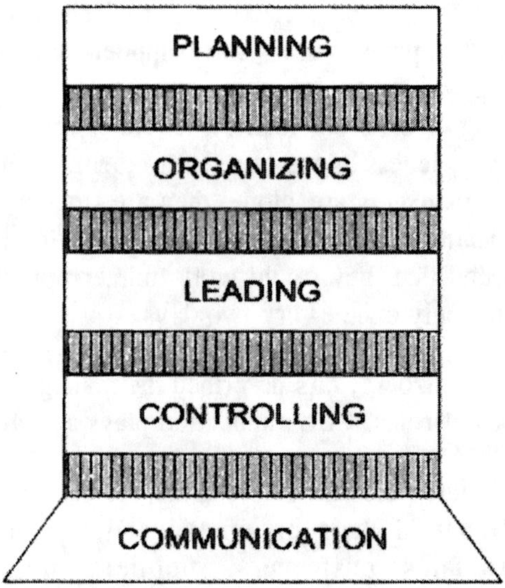

Fig. 1.5. Communication - the Foundation of Management.

1.8 Objectives of Communication

The objectives of communication are:

1. To develop information and understanding.

2. To foster any attitude which is necessary for motivation, co-operation and job satisfaction.

3. To discourage misinformation, ambiguity and rumors.

4. To prepare people for a change in methods or environment by giving them the necessary information in advance.

5. To encourage communicatee to supply ideas and suggestions and taking these suggestions seriously.

6. In an organisation to improve management relations by keeping the communication channels open.

7. To encourage social relations among people by encouraging intercommunication.

1.9 Communication Elements

Elements of Speaking

- Body language
- Voice Quality
- Intention
- Manner: directness, sincerity
- Dress and clothing (style, color, appropriateness for situation)
- Visual aids, animation
- Eye contact
- Emotional content, energy strength
- Self concept
- Concept of others
- Listening, hearing the underlying message
- Speaking from the heart
- Energy
- Setting, time, place, timing

- How the messenger holds the message
- Sensitivity
- Rhythm and pacing
- Attitude and confidence
- Rapport
- Agenda
- Purpose of communication-knowing what you want to communicate
- Clarity
- Silence, centering, looking.

Elements of Listening

- Attentiveness to speaker
- Eye contact
- Intention be fully awake and aware
- Openness: to other person and your own
- Paying attention
- Listening to yourself
- Feedback
- Body language
- Change in pattern.

1.10 Summary

In general, communication plays a very important role among friends, within the family, in all social circles and organisations. Effective management of an organisation is a function of effective communication. Communication plays an important role in all walks of human life as well as organisational life.

Communication leads to greater effectiveness, gets people involved with organisation, increases motivation to perform well and increases commitment to the organisation. In everyday life it makes for better understanding and relationships.

Dance is the unique form of communication that involves patterns, movement and creativity. It is the highest and most unique form of human expressions, so is communication. Both have number of similarities viz. multipurpose use, co-ordination of meanings, co-orientation, patterned activity etc. There are some communication situations that require more specialised skills, but as with dance one can refine and improve his/her skills. Communication is effective only when the people to whom you communicate - receives your message - understands it - remembers it and responds to it. Communication is the foundation of management function. It plays a vital role in a manager's job in his interpersonal, informational and decisional roles. Developing information's and understanding, fostering positive attitude, taking suggestions, improving management relations, encouraging social relations and discouraging misinformation's and rumors are some of the objectives that can be achieved through better communication.

2

Communication Process

The communication process is the method of transmitting information from the sender to receiver and being able to get a feedback. Between the first stage of the information being sent from the source there is the message, channels, sometimes noise and we will know the communication was effective when the receiver responds to the message.

2.1 The Communication Process

The simplest model of the communication process may be represented as:

Sender ⟶ Message ⟶ Receiver

The model indicates three essential elements of communication, obviously, if one of the elements is missing, no communication can take place. For example, we can send a message, but if it is not heard or received by someone, no communication has occurred.

Unfortunately, this simple model does not suggest the complexity of the communication process. Most of us, for example, are familiar with the game of "telephone" in which one person whispers a message into the ear of another. That person whispers the message to another, and so on. Inevitably, when the last person says the message out loud, it is quite different from what had first been whispered. "Telephone" illustrates one complexity in the communication process: The sender may send a message, but the receiver may "hear" or receive a message the sender did not intend.

To communicate well, we need to know our frames of reference and ourselves and to be able to assess other people. Only then can we hope to find the best ways in which to communicate effectively with them, both to pass information and build leadership. Some of the reasons we do not assess other people well are given below:

- We assume that they are going to behave the same way in every situation.
- We try too hard to put everyone into consistent categories (Stereotyping).
- We are too influenced by first impressions.
- We are positively influenced where we have common transmit characteristics with other people, e.g., same school, same function, same organisation.
- We are too influenced by apparent negative points, e.g., if someone is not very good at short term decision making, we might assume that he/she is not going to be good at long-term planning either.
- We make constant errors because of our own limited frames of reference and self-concept.
- We are not sufficiently interested in, or pay enough attention to, other people.

All of the above can cause us considerable problems in the communication process that consists of basically in four phases:

- Sending (via symbols)
- Receiving (via symbols)

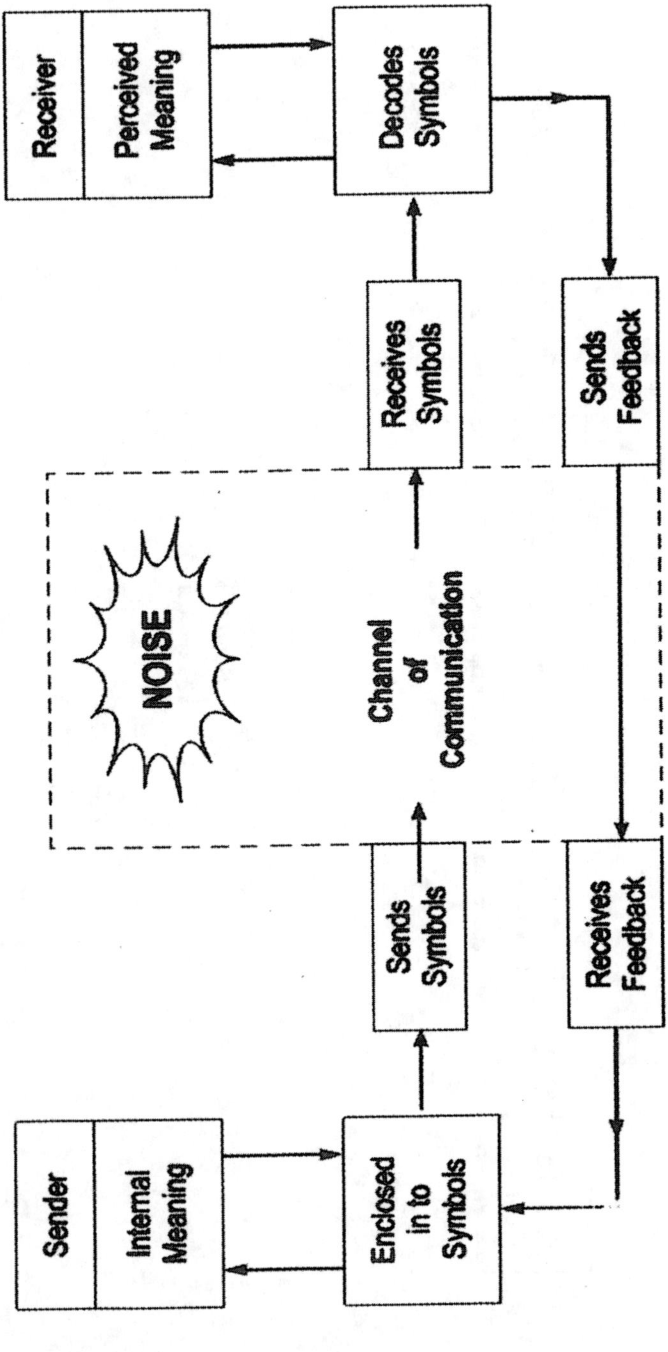

Fig. 2.1. Model of the Communication Process.

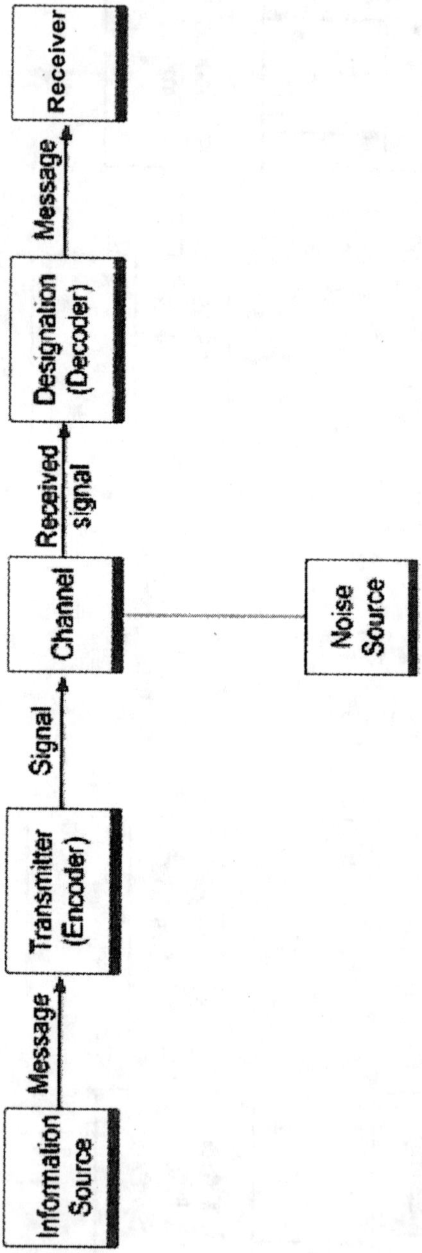

Fig. 2.2. Shannon and Weaver Model.

- Understanding (perceived meaning)
- Accepting (using feedback).

These are as shown in the following model of communication process:

"Shannon and Weaver" model, (Fig. 2.2) was developed to help engineers decide how to most efficiently transmit electrical impulses from one place to another. Other models having a more social-psychological emphasis were developed based on Shannon and Weaver's (1949) basic premise. As fascinating as these models are the purpose is not to provide a through exegesis on them. Rather the point is that in this class of models, communication is not only visually represented as a one-way activity but also conceptually proclaimed to be so.

Typical models of communication look like the one shown in Fig. 2.3. Note that the context is pictured as an element outside the communicators. The implication is that two people share and operate in the same context. It is as if the context is like air: breathed by everyone, walked through by everybody, and existing

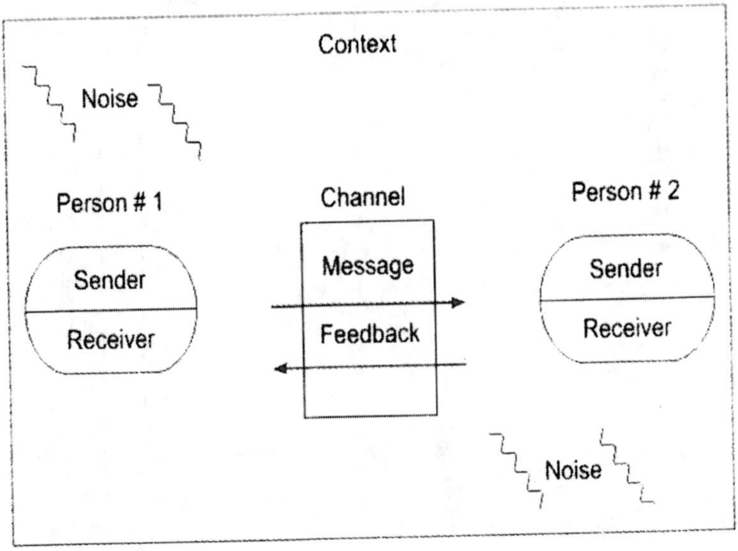

Fig. 2.3. Shannon and Weaver Model of Communication Process.

A MODEL OF THE COMMUNICATION PROCESS

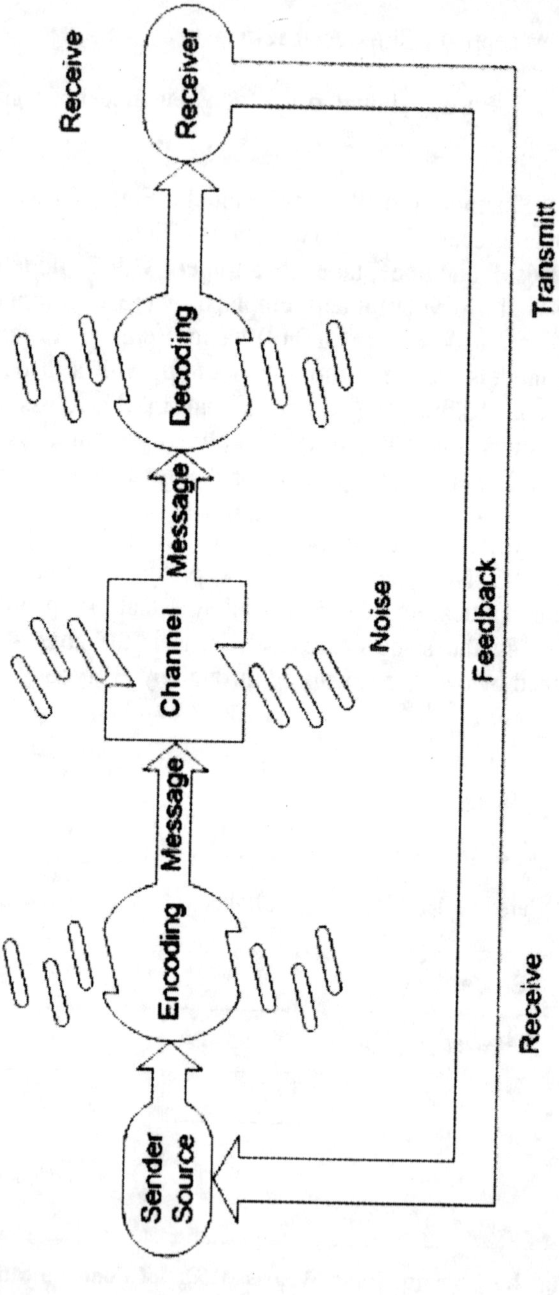

Fig. 2.4.

independent of anyone's presence. This is wrong. There is not one context, there are many. A context is not walked into; rather it is carried around in the minds of individuals. Context is not some kind of ever-present either, but a function of complex interactions between people and the setting. Our culture clearly shapes our perceptions, but fundamentally each individual has a personal and uniquely configured context. In short, context is a self-constructed image of the world.

We will describe of a far more sophisticated model of communication process as shown below and discuss each major element.

Sender Source

The sender, or source of the message, initiates the communication. In an organisation, the sender will be a person with information, needs or desires and a purpose for communicating them to one or more other people. A manager watches to communicate information about an important production deadline for the purpose of motivating other members of the department. A production line worker speaks to the shop supervisor for the purpose of requesting additional help with a project. Without a reason, purpose, or desire the sender has no need to send.

Encoding

Encoding takes place when the sender translates the information to be transmitted into a series of symbols. Encoding is necessary because information can only be transferred from one person to another through representations or symbols. Since communication is the object of encoding, the sender attempts to establish "mutuality" of meaning with the receiver by choosing symbols, usually in the form of words and gestures that the sender believes to have the same meaning for the receiver. Lack of mutuality is one of the most common causes of misunderstanding or lack of communication. In Bulgaria and some parts of India, for example, "NO" is indicated with a side-to-side shake of the head, while; "YES" is indicated with a nod. Visiting foreigners who do not share these symbols can quickly experience when they talk with citizens of these areas. Misunderstandings may also result from subtle differences in mutuality.

Gestures, too, may be subject to different interpretations. A worker in a noisy factory may convey to a co-worker that he wants a machine to be shut off by drawing his hand, palm down, across his neck in a "cut-throat" gesture. If one walked up to a police officer and made the same gesture, a different reaction might result. Even raising one's eyebrows can have varying meanings, expressing surprise in one context and skepticism in another.

Message

The message is the physical form into which the sender encodes the information. The message may be in any form that can be experienced and understood by one or more of the senses of the receiver. Speech may be heard: written words may be read; gestures may be seen or felt. A touch of the hand may communicate messages ranging from comfort to menace. A wave of the hand can communicate widely diverse messages depending on the number of fingers extended. Nonverbal messages are an extremely important form of communication, since they are often more honest or meaningful than oral or written messages. For example, a manager who frowns while saying "Good morning" to a late-arriving subordinate is clearly communicating something more than a polite greeting.

Channel

The channel is the method of transmission from one person to another (such as air for spoken words and paper for letters); it is often inseparable from the message. For communication to be effective and efficient, the channel must be appropriate for the message. A phone conversation would be an unsuitable channel for transmitting a complex engineering diagram, overnight express mail might be more appropriate. The needs and requirements of the receiver must also be considered in selecting a channel. An extremely complicated message, for example, should be transmitted in a channel that permits the receiver to refer to it repeatedly.

Although managers have a broad array of channels available to them, they may not always use the one that is most effective. Their choices may be guided by habit or personal preference. One person may use the telephone because he or she dislikes writing;

another may continue to use handwritten memos when electronic mail would be much more efficient. Both modes are appropriate in certain circumstances, so the manager must make individual decisions for each situation.

How does one choose the best channel? Written and graphic communications, such as memos, letters, reports and blueprints, are clear and precise and provide a permanent record. The telephone and face-to-face oral communication offer the advantage of immediate feedback. In choosing the appropriate channel, then, managers must decide whether clarity or feedback is more important. Many different factors are involved in the communication process, so no single technique is always preferable to the alternatives.

Receiver

The receiver is the person whose senses, perceive the sender's message. There may be a large number of receivers, as when a memo is addressed to all the members of an organisation or there may be just one as when one discusses something privately with a colleague. The message must be drafted with the receiver's background in mind. An engineer in a microchip manufacturing company, for example, might have to avoid using technical terms in a communication with someone in the company's advertising department; by the same token, the person in advertising might find engineers unreceptive to communications about demographics. If the message does not reach a receiver, communication has not taken place. The situation is not much improved if the message reaches a receiver but the receiver doesn't understand it.

Decoding

Decoding is the process by which the receiver interprets the message and translates it into meaningful information. It is a two-step process: The receiver must first perceive the message, and then interpret it. Decoding is affected by the receiver's past experience, personal assessment of the symbols and gestures used, expectations (people tend to hear what they want to hear), and mutuality of meaning with the sender. In general, the more the receiver's decoding matches the sender's intended message, the more effective the communication has been.

Noise

Noise is any factor that disturbs, confuses, or otherwise interferes with communication. It may be internal (as when a receiver is not paying attention) or external (as when the message is distorted by other sounds in the environment). Noise can occur at any stage of the communication process. It may occur during passage through the channel, for example, a radio signal may be distorted by bad weather but most interference arises in the encoding or decoding stage.

The urge to make sense of a communication is so strong that a puzzling or even nonsensical communication is often decoded by the receiver in to a sensible statement that may have an entirely different meaning from the originally encoded message: For example, unclear instructions on how to perform a task may cause employees to "hear" different and incorrect instructions.

Since noise can interfere with understanding, managers should attempt to restrict it to a level that permits effective communication. It can be very tiring to listen to a subordinate who speaks softly on a noisy assembly line or to try to conduct a conversation over telephone.

Physical discomfort such as hunger, pain or exhaustion can also be considered a form of noise and can interfere with effective communication. The problems are made worse, of course, by message that is excessively complex or unclear to begin with. A clear message expressed in a straightforward fashion ("Turn off that radio!"), however can be conveyed even in an extremely "noisy" environment.

Feedback

Feedback is a reversal of the communication process in which a reaction to the sender's communication is expressed. Since the receiver has become the sender, feedback goes through the same steps as the original communication. Organisational feedback may be in a variety of forms, ranging from direct feedback, such as a simple spoken acknowledgment that the message has been received, to indirect feedback, expressed through actions or documentation.

For example, a straightforward request for a faster rate of production may be met directly with an assenting nod of the head or indirectly with record-breaking output or a union strike.

Feedback is optional and may exist in any degree (from minimal to complete) in any given situation. In most organisational communications, the greater the feedback, the more effective the communication process is likely to be. For example, early feedback will enable managers to know if their instructions have been understood and accepted. Without such feedback, a manager might not know (until too late) whether the instructions were accurately received and carried out.

2.2 Personality and Perception in Communication Process

There are nearly as many definitions of personality as there are psychologists! From Freudian sexual repression to Jungian self-actualisation to Adlers superiority complex. What we need to know about personality as managers is that we are not born with it, at least, not totally. For personality is determined and developed by both the influences of our inherited genes and of our social and physical environment and experiences. These give us our unique individual core values, beliefs and needs which shape our consistent behaviour to the world. Once we have reached a level of psychological maturity, our personalities do not change very much and their components are integrated- What it does mean is that as we all have different experiences in life, and rarely have the same physical and social environment as others, the combination of inherited and environmental factors which interact with each other in complex ways results in patterns of behaviour which are unique to us as individuals. So we vary in intelligence, education, religious beliefs, social background and experiences, and this affects the way we communicate with others.

All these factors create individually different frames of reference, with the result that each person looks at the world in a particular and unique way. Our physical and mental make-up and our environment directly affect our perception and judgment. Perception is the process by which we select, organise and interpret sensory stimuli and information in terms which are consistent with our own frames of reference and view of the world. We are continually receiving information. Some of it we ignore, some we accept and interpret in the light of our past experience to forecast, as accurately as possible, what is going to happen in the future. In this way we form images of people, often based on very little information, predict their behaviour in certain situations, and select what, in our view, is the best way to approach, influence or communicate with them. Too often, when interpreting information, we see or hear what we expect to see or hear, rather than dealing with objective facts. The biggest barrier to objectivity is our self-concept, what we know are in relation to the world and other people and we tend to reject information which appears to threaten our self-concept.

As we are all different and our perceptions are different the process of communicating effectively with other people is rather difficult at times. It is easier when we get to know and understand people: where there is unshared perception, values and understanding, effective communication is unlikely. How many times at a first meeting have you thought, I don't like this fellow, I can't get through to him? First impressions tend to last, as we tend to reject cues to the contrary when they are threatening to our confidence in judging people.

Fig. 2.5 illustrates how to increase objectivity in the way we perceive others, and how to increase self-knowledge. The Joehari Window (shown in Fig. 2.5) is useful in reducing, perceptual bias in interpersonal perception. When we are with other people there are some elements of ourselves, our attitudes, behaviour and personality with which we are familiar and which are also apparent to others (the OPEN area). Similarly, other people may observe facet of ourselves of which we are unaware, e.g., 'he's bad breath' (the BLIND area). We also tend to keep some of ourselves, our attitudes and feelings, private and do not disclose to others (the HIDDEN area). And we also know. That there are some aspects of ourselves which we do not understand and which are not apparent to others but which do affect our behaviour such as flying into a blind range for no reason at all (the unknown area).

	Known to Self	*Unknown to Self*
Known to others	Open	Blind
Unknown to others	Hidden	Unknown

Fig. 2.5.

When we first meet someone, we tend not to reveal much about ourselves - our open area is small. This often leads to first impressions of us, which are wrong. For communication to be effective, we need jointly to work with others to increase the size of the open area, while reducing the blind and hidden areas. This can be achieved by two conscious sets of activities - self disclosure and feedback. Self-disclosure is giving free information ourselves to others, so reducing the hidden area, and from others reduces the size of the blind area. When both are used, it can also help to reduce the size of the unknown, and reveal some of our underlying motives.

Summary

The simplest form of communicating process is

Sender à Message à Receiver.

If either of the elements is missing, no communication takes place. Communication process basically consists of four phases:

- Sending (via Symbols - Encoding);
- Receiving (via Symbols Decoding);
- Understanding (perceived meaning);
- Accepting (using feedback)

'Shanon and Weaver' communication model represents the communication as a one-way activity. But the typical communication model stresses the importance of 'context' in communication. People differ in their experiences, so they perceive differently. Each individual has a uniquely configured context - the self-constructed image of the world. So the understanding differs from individual to individual for the same message. A far more sophisticated model has included almost all the important elements in communicating process viz; Sender, Encoding, Message, Channel, Decoding, Noise, Feedback, etc. Each element influences the communicating process.

3

Communication Modes

Communication, whether in organisations, personal relationships, politics or public information campaigns, is one of the most complex and strategic activities of human beings. It may have limited effectiveness for two interacting reasons. This chapter elaborates various modes and strategies of communication those play key role in improvising the effectiveness.

3.1 Communication in Organisation

An organisation consists of a number of people that involves interdependence. If you had 1,000 people, each of whom designed a product, purchased materials, manufactured, sold and distributed the product, you would not have an organisation, you would have 1,000 enterprises. People are interdependent when the performance of one individual affects and is affected by the performance of others: for example, when one person designs the product, another purchased materials, and so on. Interdependence calls for coordination of activities that ensures that individual tasks will be carried out so that the objectives of the organisation will be achieved. And coordination requires communication.

With the acceleration of the efficient use of information technology, the nature of managerial relationships is changing. Managers of the future may have fewer subordinates but rely more on information system. Relationships between colleagues then become more critical to the success of the organisation as information needs to be transferred and integrated across internal boundaries. So, as a manager's role in gathering and passing information increases, his skills as an interpersonal communicator will determine his effectiveness.

So we will be concentrating primarily, on people communicating with other people within it.

Communication in organisations uses two basic channels - formal, and informal. Both are important and both carry messages - sometimes reinforcing, sometimes conflicting throughout the organisation. Formal channels are ones that have been set up by the organisation - Messages flow in three directions: downwards, upwards and sideways. The downward messages consist primarily of information that is necessary for any staff to carryout their work, such as policies and procedures, orders and requests which are passed down to the appropriate level in the hierarchy. Upwards messages are reports, requests, opinions, complaints. Sideways messages are between different departments, functions or people at the same level in the organisation.

There tend to be strict rules about the use of these formal. For communication to be effective, all three channels to be open and unblocked at all times. The upward channel one, which blocks most easily, and when this happens it is indicator that an organisation's policies, procedures and employee relations need to be reviewed.

Informal channels spring up by virtue of common interests between people in organisations, these interests may be caused by work, social or outside relationships. The grapevine is a very powerful channel and has been estimated that managers receive over half the information they need for planning purposes through the grapevine. Its messages may frequently be distorted, but fhey often carry more credibility than those coming through formal channels. And it's quicker! One Managing Director said if I plant a rumor, one knows that I will get a reaction within a day. If I send a formal memo, it takes three weeks before I get a response. Informal channels often become the only means of communication when formal channels become blocked or break down.

Effective communication in organisations, like effective communication anywhere, still involves getting an accurate message from one person to another (or perhaps to several people). Unclear organisational communication can make a complex idea or process completely unintelligible. However, several factors unique to organisations influence the effectiveness of communication; *viz.*:

1. The formal channels of communication influence communication effectiveness in two ways. First, the formal channels cover an ever-widening distance as organisations develop and grow. For example, effective communication is usually far more difficult to achieve in a large retail organisation with widely dispersed branches than in a small department store. Second, the formal channels of communication inhibit the free flow information between organisational levels. An assembly line worker, for example, will almost always communicate problems to a supervisor rather than to the plant manager, this accepted restriction in the channels of communication has its advantages.

2. The organisation's authority structure has a similar influence on communication effectiveness. Status and power differences in the organisation help determine who will communicate comfortably with whom. The content and accuracy of the communication will also be affected by authority differences among individuals. For example, conversation between a company president and a clerical worker may well be characterised by somewhat strained politeness and formality; neither party is likely to say much of importance.

3. Job specialisation usually facilitates communication within differentiated groups. Members of the same work group are likely to share the same jargon of time horizons, goals, tasks, and personal styles. Communication between highly differentiated groups, however, is likely to be inhibited.

4. The term information ownership means that individuals possess unique information and knowledge about their jobs. A darkroom employee, for example, may have found a particularly efficient way to develop photo prints; a department head may have a particularly effective way of handling conflict among subordinates; a salesperson may know who the key decision makers are in his or her major accounts. Such information is a form of power for the individuals who possess it; they are able to function more effectively than their peers. Many individuals with such skills and knowledge are unwilling to share this information with others. As a result, completely open communication within the organisation does not take place.

Communication Networks Within the Organisation

Some very interesting research has been carried out on communication channels in organisations and their effects on communication accuracy; task performance, and group member satisfaction. This research is particularly important because managers have some influence over how communication channels develop in their units. For example, the formal authority structure that managers establish will help determine who will interact with whom. Thus, managers can design their work units to facilitate effective communication.

Organisations can design their communication networks or structures in a variety of ways. Some communication networks may be rigidly designed. For example, employees can be discouraged from talking with anyone except their immediate supervisor. Such a network is usually intended to keep higher-level managers free from being overburdened with unnecessary information and to maintain the higher-level managers' power and status. Other networks may be more loosely designed. Individuals may be encouraged to communicate with anyone at any level. Such networks may be used wherever a free flow of information is highly desirable, as in a research department.

Vertical Communication

Vertical communication consists of communication up and down the organisation chain of command. Downward communication starts with top management and flows down through management levels to line workers and non-supervisory personnel. The major purpose of downward communication are to advise, inform, direct, instruct, and evaluate subordinates and to provide organisation members with information about organisational goals and policies.

The main function of upward communication is to supply information to the upper levels about what is happening at the lower levels. This type of communication includes progress reports, suggestions, explanation and requests for aid or decisions.

Problems of Vertical Communication

Downward communication is likely to be filtered, modified, or halted at each level as managers decide what should be passed down to their subordinates. Upward communication is likely to be filtered, condensed, or altered by middle managers who see it, as part of their job to protect upper management from nonessential data originating at the lower levels. In addition, middle managers may keep information that would reflect unfavourably on them from reaching their superiors. Thus, vertical communication is often at least partially inaccurate or incomplete. The importance to an organisation of vertical communication was Emphasised by a survey of research conducted by Lyman W. Porster and Karlene H. Roberts, who reported that two thirds of a manager's communication takes place with superiors and subordinates. The studies reviewed by Porter and Roberts also found that the accuracy of vertical communication was aided by similarities in thinking between superior and subordinate. But it was limited by status and power differences between manager and subordinate, by a subordinate's desire for upward mobility, and by a lack of trust between manager and subordinate. For example, some studies suggest that communication is likely to be less open and accurate, the higher the subordinates' aspirations for upward mobility. Such subordinates are likely to be ambitious, strongly opinionated, forceful, and aggressive and consequently are more concerned with defending their self-image than in reaching and in agreement or an objectively accurate appraisal of a situation. They are also less likely to communicate reports that may be interpreted as negative comments on their performance of ability. Subordinates are also more likely to screen out problems, disagreements, or complaints when they feel that their superior has the power to punish them.

Even unambitious subordinates will be guarded in their communications if an atmosphere of trust does not exist between them and their superiors. Subordinates conceal or distort information if they feel that their superiors cannot be trusted to be fair or that they may use the information against them. The net result of these communication problems is that higher-level managers frequently make decisions based on faulty or inadequate information.

Problems in downward communication exist when managers do not provide subordinates with the information they need to carry out their tasks effectively. Managers are often overly optimistic about the accuracy and completeness in downward communication; in fact, they frequently fail to pass on important information (such as a higher level change in policy) or to instruct subordinates adequately on how to perform their duties. This lack of communication is sometimes deliberate, as when managers withhold information to keep subordinates dependent on them. The net effect of incomplete, downward communication is that subordinates may feel confused, uninformed or powerless and may fail to carry out their tasks properly.

Lateral Communication

Lateral communication usually follows the pattern of work; flow in an organisation, occurring between members of work groups, between one work group and another, between members of different departments, and between line and staff. The main purpose of lateral communication is to provide a direct channel for organisational coordination and problem solving. In this way, it avoids the much slower procedure of directing communications through a common superior. An added benefit of lateral communication is that it enables organisation members to form relationships with their peers. These relationships are an important part of employee satisfaction.

3.1.1 One-way and Two-way Communication

Communication may be one-way or two-way. In one-way communication the sender communicates without expecting or getting feedback from the receiver. Policy statements from top managers are usually examples of one-way communication. Two-way communication exists when the receiver provides feedback to the sender. Making a suggestion to a subordinate and receiving a question or counter-suggestion is an example of two-way communication.

Harold Leavitt and Ronald Mueller conducted early experiments on the effects and effectiveness of one way and two-way communication. In these experiments, individuals were asked to describe an arrangement of geometric shapes to groups of listeners. They were to use words only. The listeners were asked to reproduce the diagrams from the verbal descriptions. The experiments were conducted under conditions of one-way communication and two-way communications. In the one-way communication, the sender could not see or hear the listeners. In the two-way experiment, descriptions were still limited to words but the sender was allowed to face the listeners and could question or comment freely. The result of the experiments were as follows:

1. One-way communication takes considerably less time than two-way communication.

2. Two-way communication is more accurate than one-way communication. (That is the diagrams were more accurately reproduced when two-way communication was used.) The feedback allows the sender to refine his or her communication for the receivers so that it becomes more precise and accurate.

3. Receivers are surer of themselves and of their judgments when two-way communications is used. The very fact that they are permitted to ask questions probably increases the receiver's self-confidence. In addition they can use questions to clarify any doubts they may have.

4. Sender can easily feel attacked when two-way communication is used because receivers will call attention to the sender's ambiguities and mistakes.

5. Although it is less accurate one-way communication appears much more orderly than two-way communication, which often appears noisy and chaotic.

As Leavitt has pointed out, these results can provide guidelines for communication in organisations. If communication must be fast and accuracy is easy to achieve, one-way communication is both more economical and more efficient. If orderliness is considered vital as in a large, public meeting one-way communication might also be more appropriate. One-way communication also has political benefits. It reduces the chance that the sender's mistakes will be publicly revealed and challenged.

Where accuracy of communication is important, however, as in instructions for carrying out complex tasks the two-way method is almost essential. Without feedback from the receiver, the sender has little basis for judging the accuracy of the communication or the degree of understanding and comprehension experienced by the receiver.

In most situations, managers will have to create the most efficient mix of one-way and two-way communication. Some categories of managerial communications, such as straightforward statement of organisation rules and policies, require little or no feedback to assure clarity. In many other cases, such as the formulation of organisational objectives or the implementation of a new sales strategy, two-way communications is usually essential.

3.1.2 Superior-subordinate Communication

One of the basic foundations of the organisational operations is the communication between superiors and subordinates in the hierarchical system. Traditionally, the dominant theme in this type of organisational communication has been the "Downward" communications as far as the directions are concerned and "upward" communications as far as operational reports and other feedback is concerned.

The downward communication is from the superior to the subordinate or from the top management filtered down to workers through the various hierarchical communications centres in between and may include such standard managerial tools as statement of the organisational philosophy and organisational objectives, standard operating procedures, standard quality control procedures, safety regulations, and other relevant material. Downward channels are used to give employees, work instructions and other information needed to exercise the delegated authority.

In order for this communication to be effective the workers should not only be told what to do, but also why they are doing it, and why their jobs are important. This increases a feeling of acceptance on the part of workers. It is also important that the communication be transmitted to workers in the language that they can understand. For example, a machine operator may not understand much about the organisational philosophy or any specialised terminology about strategic planning or technological dynamics. They must be communicated in their own words and perceptions. Also most workers are conditioned to accept communication from their immediate superiors and hence the message must be filtered down through normal channels and edited on the way down wherever necessary without losing the content or intent of the message. It is important, however, that there is no communication breakdown at any level or from any source. This breakdown may occur due to failure of the message to get through, failure to deliver the message at the proper time or proper place or improper coding of the message. The message must be coded in the language of the receiver, rather than the language of the sender.

Subordinate-Superior Communication moves in the opposite direction and is based upon the communication demand system, designed by the management to receive information from operational levels. This information may consist of standard reporting items such as production reports, sales reports, customer complaints, quality control reports etc. According to Ester R Becker, upward communication provides a clear channel for funneling information, opinion and attitudes up through the organisation. The organisation must provide a climate and an incentive system, which is necessary to encourage such communication. This climate can be generated by an "open door" policy where the workers know that their superiors are always available for discussion of problems. This opportunity for upward communication encourages employees to contribute valuable ideas for improving organisational efficiency.

Wenburg Wilmoat suggests that instead of communication being "upward" or "downward" which is inter-communication, it should be "transactional" communication which is mutual and reciprocal because, "All persons are engaged in sending (encoding) and receiving (decoding) messages simultaneously. Each person is constantly sharing in the encoding and decoding process and each person is affecting the other one. In the transactional process the communication is not simply flow of information, but it develops a personal linkage between the superior and the subordinate.

There are five purposes served by superior-subordinate communication process. These are:

- To give specific job instructions and directions.
- To give information about organisational procedures and practices.
- To educate employees as to why their jobs are important.
- To give feedback to subordinates about their performance as to how well they are doing and how they can improve.
- To provide ideological type information to facilitate the indoctrination of goals.

It has been found that in most classical types of organisations only the first two of these five purposes are generally accomplished. Attention to the other three purposes has a very positive impact upon the organisational climate.

In order to achieve these five communication purposes effectively, it is necessary to have effective superior-subordinate communication, which requires a careful attention to the needs and the psychology of the receiver. The importance of the receiver should not be ignored. Donald Roberts has suggested the following ways in which the downward flow of communication can affect the receiver.

- People's interpretations of communications coincide with the already held beliefs and attitudes.

- People usually resist messages and communications that require sudden changes.
- Messages that require some kind of change are more easily acceptable if the entire surrounding environment is also changing alongside.
- Messages that conflict with values of the receivers will not be acceptable even if these messages are rational and logically desirable.
- Messages that fulfill some needs of the receiver will be more easily acceptable.

Based on these observations, it is important that the superior and subordinate work together and have a personal linkage along with professional relationship.

3.1.3 Inter-departmental Communication

Departments in an organisation are what rooms are to a house. Departments divide. Department's separate. Department's specialise. And departments create barriers. The word "Department" comes from the Middle French word "Departir" which means to separate. Four particular "Separations" are critical when examining interdepartmental communication problems.

- First, generally, departments perform separate functions;
- Second, generally, departments are physically separated;
- Third, typically departments are separated through accounting procedures;
- Fourth, departments separate employees through the authority structure.

How can interdepartmental communication problems be effectively managed? Of paramount importance is management's commitment to effective communication between departments. They must be committed not only to short-term projects but also to long-term structural changes. The communication system must not be overly constrained.

To ease inter-departmental communication problems, managers must seek to balance two counteracting forces, just as a dancer balances creative impulse within musical constraints. One tension point could be called the "sender's concerns, "because an effective communication system avoids wasting the time of information providers. It is counterproductive for a system to be so open that employees are expected to answer the same question 10 to 15 times a day. Employees get weary answering the same questions day after day, especially when the information is readily available in a written form. The second tension point could be termed the "inquirer's concerns." Employees need sufficient information to get their job done. Hence, the system needs to be open enough to answer and process legitimate information requests.

The perfect system would block all redundant information requests but allow every unique or special inquiry-this ideal will no doubt prove elusive, but as a starting point, department managers

Table 3.1. Constraints in Sharing Information

Information Providers Concerns	*Information Consumers Concerns*
• Answering questions takes time.	• Information is needed to complete tasks.
• Information dissemination is a responsibility.	• Sometimes it is easier to call or ask someone than look up the answer.
• My priority should be answering non-routine inquiries.	• Sometimes a routine request for information is a way to legitimately get someone's attention I couldn't normally contact.
• Providing information also facilitates receiving information.	• They might tell me something I don't know.
• It takes time to document everything.	• I just want to make sure the information is current. I want to confirm the written information.

need to be aware of the inherent tension between the concerns of senders and inquirers. The objective is to develop sensitivity to the needs, desires, and problems of other departments/After all today's requester may be tomorrow's provider. Frustration by either party ultimately results in discontent for all.

Most organisations to some degree have difficulties with interdepartmental communication. Unfortunately, the problem frequently is overlooked and, even when recognise, often the symptoms are treated instead of the causes.

Avoiding unnecessary conflict, low performance, time delays, and decisions that work at cross-purposes are compelling reasons for taking active measures to improve interdepartmental communication. Yet one question remains: At what cost? Are there any dangers in encouraging interdepartmental communication? In a word, yes. An overly integrated organisation can stifle creativity and innovation, and develop a tendency for "groupthink". Frankly, given the ingrained belief in the wisdom departmentalisation, these possibilities are remote.

The other disadvantage of this is time. As many Japanese businesses have discovered, decisions typically will take more time to make because all the departments have to be consulted and allowed input in to an impending change. But that time often is more than compensated for by swift and smooth implementation. Nevertheless, a more rigidly departmentalised organisation will frequently be able to react more quickly than one that is not.

On the balance, though, the benefits of effective interdepartmental communications far exceed the costs, misunderstandings can be reduced, antagonisms avoided, cooperation encouraged, and sensitivity promoted. And in the end, a supportive communication climate can be developed and maintained.

So too, communication between departments seeks to enrich the lives of individuals throughout the entire organisation.

3.1.4 Interpersonal Communication

Communication 'is one of those words like organisation'. It is no easy to define. One way of looking at it is as an interpersonal process of sending and receiving symbols with meanings attached to them. It is, therefore, supposed to result in the exchange of information and share understanding between people. So a measure of the effective management of interpersonal communication is that information is passed, and relationships are built.

The success of information passing depends very much on the nature and quality of the information received and this in turn depends on the nature and quality of the relationship between the persons involved. People tend to experience personal satisfaction when communicating and interacting with friends, relatives and others they know well, in fact, with people with whom they feel comfortable. They don't feel the need to be guarded because of the way they manage their relationships with each other. They can speak openly and honestly and joke about serious matters. Personal abuse is a form of comradeship. But managers frequently have to work with others with whom they have not developed close relationships in order to achieve organisational objectives. Misunderstandings may occur, leading to disagreement and conflict, or often the avoidance of conflict and the development of mistrust. Out of this can develop lack of co-operation and an unhealthy work climate. People are polite to each other, and apparently genuinely co-operative. But because the understanding interpersonal problems have not been faced, the quality of interpersonal communication is poor.

People are different, and we need to understand the nature of those differences and try to modify our interpersonal behaviour to cope with them. You, as an individual, may have a consistent view of the world, your organisation and your job, but you have to work in an environment consisting of other people. That is your dilemma. In reality, one of your greatest challenges as a manager is that other people are different from you. Two of the basic differences between people are personality and perception. These differences caused people to behave differently towards others in different situations, and cause communication problems.

Our definition of interpersonal communication calls attention to three essential points:

- That communication, as we are using the terms, involves people, and that understanding communication, therefore involves trying to understand how people relate to each other;

- That communication involves shared meaning, which suggest that in order for people to communicate, they must agree on the definitions of the terms they are using; and

- That communication is symbolic-gestures, sounds, letters, numbers and words can only represent or approximate the ideas they are meant to communicate.

At the senior level, interpersonal communication skill assumes greater significance. How can you get round the people, how can you get on with people and even get over people. So this understanding of people and working with them is the skill required at the senior level.

Related Concepts in Interpersonal Communication

Conversation: Often considered informal and everyday speech, but more formally a finite element within an ongoing relationship based on interpersonal communication. Most conversations of a standard five-step process of opening, built-up, substance, feedback, and closing. Since a conversation is a two-way process, it involves various controls, many associated with conversational turns (the changing of the speaker and listener role). Conversations can exist in both direct and mediated settings.

Speech act: An intentional utterance made to achieve an intended goal. In an informal context, a speech act might be a promise made by a parent to his or her child. A more formal example of a speech act is an interview given by a government leader with hopes of persuading voters.

Communication competence: The ability to communicate in a socially acceptable way. For interpersonal relationships, this involves the speaker's interaction with others. For more public situations, this involves the audience perception of the speaker in terms of vocal presentation, message control, command of language, physical appearance, and so on.

Self-disclosure: Process of making internal revelations about oneself that others would be unlikely to know otherwise. While self-disclosure is an individual communication tactic, it invites reciprocity.

Gender differences: Communication scholars have researched the varying ways men and women communicate, which often varies further among different cultures. Some of the major differences are that men use report talk to share information or demonstrate knowledge, whereas women often use rapport talk to enhance relationships and share experiences. Psychologists have observed that men and women who are androgynous in their communication styles rather than those who rely heavily on stereotypically masculine or feminine style are more successful in their interactions with others.

Meta-communication: Communication about the act or process of communicating rather than focusing on the content of communication. For example, a couple that argues about how to spend their money is communicating. A couple that discusses how they argue is engaging in meta-communication.

3.1.5 Intrapersonal Communication

Intrapersonal communication takes place within a single person often for the purpose of clarifying ideas or analysing a situation. Other times interpersonal communication is undertaken in order to reflect upon or appreciate some thing these aspects of interpersonal communication are – self-concept, perception and expectation.

- **Self-concept** - is the basis for interpersonal communication because it determines how a person sees him/ herself and is oriented towards others. Self-concept also called self-awareness involves three factors - beliefs, values and attitudes. Beliefs are basic personal contention towards what is true or false, good or bad, beliefs can be deceptive or perceptive. Values are deep-seated orientations and ideals generally based on and consistent with believes about right and wrong ideas and actions. Attitudes are learned pre-disposition toward or against topic ideas that stem from and generally are consistent with values. Attitudes often are global typically emotional. Beliefs, values and attitudes all influence behaviour, which can be either spoken opinion or physical action. Some physiologists include body image as an aspect of interpersonal communication, in that body image is a way of perceiving ourselves, positively/ negatively according to the social standards of our culture. Other things that affect self-concept are personal attitudes, talents, social role even births order.

- Whereas self-concept focuses internally, perception looks outward. Perception of the outside world also is rooted in beliefs, values and attitudes. It is so closely intertwined with self-concept that one feeds off the other, creating a harmonious understanding of both oneself and one's world.

- Meanwhile, expectations are future-oriented messages dealing with long-term roles, sometimes called life scripts. These sometimes are projections of learned relationships within the family or society.

Intrapersonal communication may involve different levels of communication activity: internal discourse, solo vocal communication, and solo written communication.

- Internal discourse involves thinking, concentration and analysis. Psychologists include both daydreaming and nocturnal dreaming in this category. Prayer, contemplation and meditation also are part of this category, though from a theological point of view the argument may be made that this is not solely internal to one person. In Sufi tradition, this is similar to the concept of naps, negotiating with the inner self. Example: Consciously appreciating the beauty of sunset.

- Solo vocal communication includes speaking aloud to oneself. This may be done to clarify thinking, to rehearse a message intended for others, or simply to let off steam. Example: Talking to yourself as you complain about your boss.

- Solo written communication deals with writing not intended for others. Example: An entry in a diary or personal journal.

3.1.6 Communication Grapevine

While is it necessary to have a formal organisational structure for communication channels, since an effective network and flow of communication may, "regulate behaviour, encourage innovations, integrate or coordinate activities and inform or instruct employees". It is also very beneficial to attend to informal channels of communication, commonly known as grapevine, which can communicate important organisational matters to the management that would not be feasible through formal channels.

This type of communication is more lateral in nature and is build around the social relationship and social interaction among the members of the organisation. The informal communication can be considered as a beneficial safety valve capable of carrying important information's quickly and accurately. It can also be considered as destructive, focusing on its capacity to spread rumors, destroy moral, misinform and create interpersonal problems. Such consideration will depend upon the type of climate that exists in the organisation.

The grapevine in organisations is made up of several informal communication networks that overlap and interact at a number of points that is, some well informed individuals are likely to belong to more than one informal network. Grapevines show admirable disregard for rank or authority and many link organisation members in any combination of directions - horizontal, vertical, ad diagonal, (as shown in Fig. 3.1). As Keith Davis puts it, the grapevine flows around water coolers, down hall ways, through lunch rooms and wherever people get together in groups the grapevine should not be confused with legitimate information that management seeks to transmit by word of mouth. However, when such information is transmitted by word of mouth, people at the lowest level of organisations are least likely to receive it accurately. For this reason manager who wish to ensure that the lowest level of employees receive certain information often communicate in writing.

In addition to its social and informal communication functions the grapevine has several work related functions as well. For example, although the grapevine is hard to control with any

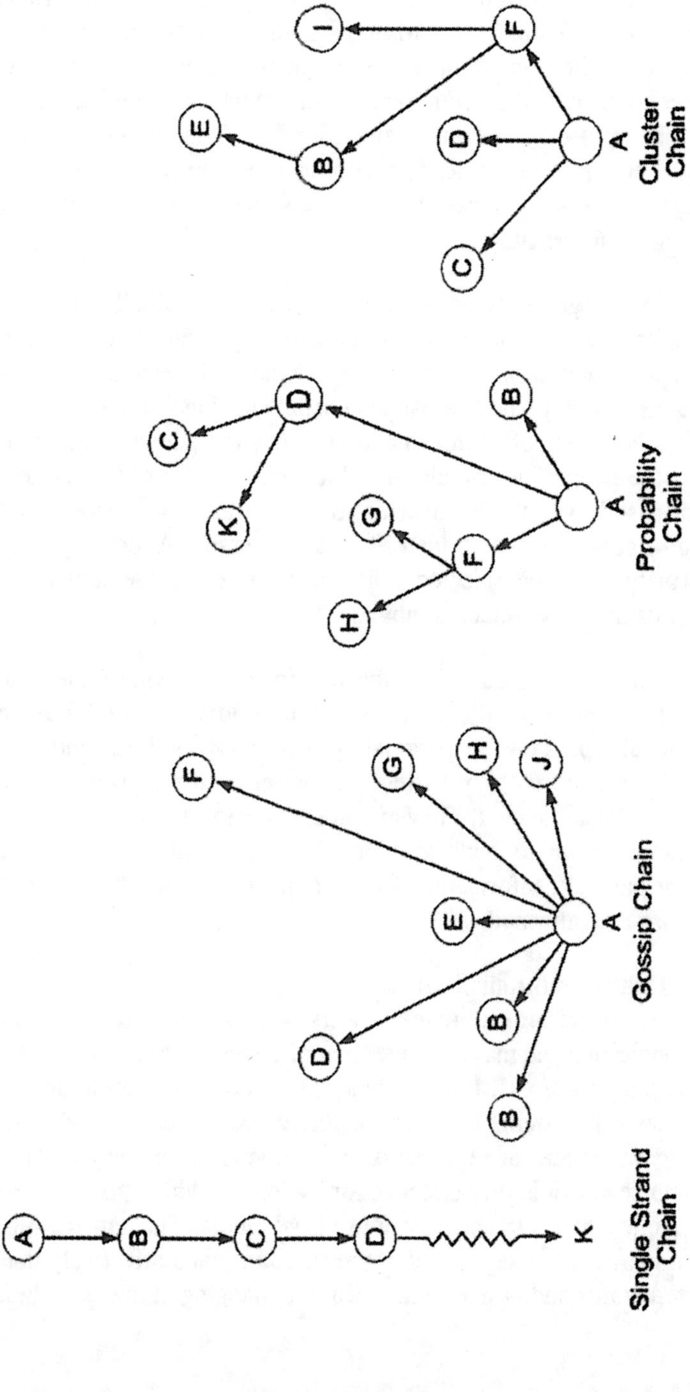
Single Strand Chain
K
Gossip Chain
A
Probability Chain
A
Cluster Chain
A

Fig. 3.1.

precision, it is often much faster in operation than formal communication channels. Managers may use it to distribute information through planned "leaks" or judiciously placed "just-between-you and me" remarks. Keith Davis has identified four possible types of grapevine chains (See Fig. 3.1). In the "Single-strand" chain, person A tells something to person B, who tells it to person C, and so on down the line. This chain is least accurate at passing on information.

In the "gossip chain" one person seeks out and tells everyone the information he or she has obtained. This chain is often used when information of an interesting but non-job related nature is being conveyed. In the "probability chain" individuals are indifferent about whom they offer information to; they tell people at random, and those people in turn tell others at random. This chain is likely to be used when the information is mildly interesting but insignificant. In the "cluster" chain, person A conveys the information to a few selected individuals: some of those individuals then inform a few selected others.

The "cluster chain" is the dominant grapevine pattern in organisations. Usually only a few individuals called liaison individuals: pass on the information they have obtained; and they are likely to do so only to individuals they trust or from whom they would like favours. They are most likely to pass on information that is interesting to them, job-related and above all timely. People do not pass old information for fear of advertising the fact that they are not informed.

3.2 Oral Communication

An oral communication is known as face-to-face communication and may be in the form of direct talk and conversation or the public address. It also includes telephone calls or talking on the intercom system. It is most effective when settling a dispute among employees or reprimanding a worker. In one-way form of communication it is very effective for leaders to address the followers via public address system or audio-visual media. The human voice can impart the message much more forcefully and effectively than written words and is an effective way of changing attitudes, beliefs and feelings. Since, faith, trust and sincerity can be much better measured in a face-to-face conversation rather than in written words.

Advantages

- It is direct, simple, time saving and least expensive form of communication.
- It allows for feedback and spontaneous thinking.
- It helps in avoiding delays, red tape and other formalities.
- It conveys personal warmth and friendliness and it develops a sense of belonging because of personalised contacts.
- Any misunderstanding can be cleared immediately.

Disadvantages

- There is no formal record of transaction.
- If the verbal message is passed on along the hierarchical chain of command then some distortions can occur during the process.
- Lengthy and distant communications cannot be effectively conveyed verbally.
- The receiver may receive the message in his own perception and thus may misunderstand the intent of the message.
- Spontaneous responses may not be carefully thought about.
- The spirit of authority cannot be transmitted effectively in verbal transaction.
- More or less or different meaning might be conveyed by manner of speaking, tone of voice and facial expressions.

The various modes of oral communication are detailed as under:

3.2.1 Conversation as Communication

Most conversations sort of drift along; in business, this is wasteful; as a manager, you seek communication rather than chatter.

To ensure an efficient and effective conversation, there are three considerations:

- You must make your message understood.
- You must receive/understand the intended message sent to you.
- You should exert some control over the flow of the communication.

Thus, you must learn to listen as well as to speak. Those who dismiss this as a mere platitude are already demonstrating an indisposition to listening: the phrase may be trite, but the message is hugely significant to your effectiveness as a manager. If you do not explicitly develop the skill of listening, you may not hear the suggestion/information, which should launch you to fame and fortune.

3.2.2 The Art of Conversation

There is the so-called art of conversation, which also works in most social situations for the benefit of those who employ it as an art. Of course, there are certain basic rules to follow. First of all, one should not start each sentence with "I" and "me/my". This creates an unpleasant image, in other words, you might suggest that you are placed in the centre of attention, that you consider yourself to be the most important person in the world. Secondly, one should not have the monopoly of the conversation. Even if you have storytelling skills, this does not mean you are entitled to keep talking all night long.

Also, it is inadvisable to jump into conclusions after each of your interlocutor's sentence, and you should avoid speaking about general issues. If you speak too fast, or repeat an idea, even if that idea is brilliant, you might end up being ignored. Even if you are right a thousand times, it's best not to interrupt your interlocutor. And while you speak to your interlocutor, you should look him in the eyes, because if you look sideways or around you might seem dishonest or absent-minded.

You should not get agitated during the discussion and it is best not to make promises that you may easily break. Also, it's impolite to contradict somebody just to show that you are original, and to approve things you are not sure of.

In group discussions, it is good to speak less than the others. To speak very little does not mean lacking general culture and is not a sign of stupidity, but proves a strong personality. Another important thing to be remembered in order to have an artful conversation, is that you should never ask your interlocutor questions referring to negative aspects of his life or his personality or belonging to somebody that is close to your interlocutor.

3.2.3 How to be an Effective Conversationalist

One of the most crucial aspects of maintaining a good conversation is how you begin it. Opening a dialog which can only be answered in a "Yes" or a "No" can kill a conversation even before it has started. Make sure you ask open-ended questions. If you want to compliment your hostess about the food, don't just say "The food is delicious". Other than mumbling a thank you or a yes, the hostess might not say anything more, and you have lost out on a great chance to have interesting talk. Statements don't usually make good conversation starters. Instead word it like "These appetizers are heavenly! Can you tell me how you prepared them?" Now you have not only praised them, but your question will now elicit a detailed response from your hostess, which can be a great way to begin a conversation.

Body Language

Your body language is one of the first things by which people will judge you. Whenever you are talking, a smile, coupled with a positive body language will keep people listening to you. Face the other person, and avoid crossing your arms or legs. Maintain an erect posture and appear genuinely interested in what he is saying. Maintain a good eye contact. Nod every once in a while. Make sure you do not overdo these things, like smiling all too quickly, or nodding too often. These are signs that you are feigning interest in the other person, and the other person might slowly drift away from you.

Choose Interesting Topics

It's something most people overlook, and then realise they don't have anything worth talking about. This is true especially if you are meeting new people, or even attending an event where you are likely to bump into lots of friends and acquaintances. How many times does the conversation comes to a standstill, after the customary hello, because you realise you have nothing to mention except the weather? All too often, I would say! Before you leave home, read up on the current news, or better still, if you know who all you are going to meet, try to garner some information about them, their likes/dislikes, profession, etc. Remember, people like to talk about themselves. The next time you face a situation like this, venture out by asking others about the books they recently read, what sorts of movies they are interested in, or where they last went for a vacation, and the conversation will be on its course again!

Show Interest in What Others Say

During a conversation, make sure you respect the other person's feelings. Do not blabber only about yourself and things that you like, but include the others in your conversation. No one wants to continue to talk to a smart-Alec, and if you do not involve others, you are likely to lose friends. And this does not mean faking interest. You must sincerely pay attention to others. Be a good listener. Keep your eyes and ears open for all those tidbits of information coming your way, which will prove helpful in continuing the dialog. When people talk, they often disclose a lot of things about themselves, their likes, work, etc. Keep an ear out for such things, pick on them, and keep the conversation in full flow.

Another aspect to this is echoing what others have said. It's one of the simplest ways to continue a conversation. Let's say, the person you are speaking to is talking about theater, and you do not know much about it. Repeat whatever he is talking about. Whenever he mentions anything about a play, an actor, anything related to his profession, listen carefully and frame questions pertaining to aspects of the topic he is talking on. This will make the speaker feel you are sincerely interested in listening to him, and please him no end. Also make sure you keep up with their choice of words. If they use the word "profession", stick to the word. Do not replace it with "vocation" or "job". When you speak their language, people will think of you as a sensitive listener.

3.2.4 Tactful Conversation

Mr. Gabor offers these tips for using TACTFUL conversations:

- T=Think before you speak
- A=Apologize quickly when you blunder
- C=Converse, don't compete
- T=Time your comments
- F=Focus on behaviour - not on personality
- U=Uncover hidden feelings
- L=Listen for feedback

Other DO's and DON'T's to Accompany T-A-C-T-F-U-L Strategies :

DO be direct, courteous and calm

DON'T be rude and pushy

DO spare others your unsolicited advice

DON'T be patronizing, superior or sarcastic

DO acknowledge that what works for you may not work for others

DON'T make personal attacks or insinuations

DO say main points first, then offer more details if necessary

DON'T expect others to follow your advice or always agree with you

DO listen for hidden feelings

DON'T suggest changes that a person cannot easily make.

3.3 Written Communication

A written communication is put in writing and is generally in the form of instructions, letters, memos, formal reports, rules and regulations, policy manuals, information bulletins etc. These areas have to be covered in writing for efficient functioning of an organisation. It is most effective when it is required to communicate information that requires action in the future and where the communication is that of general informational nature. It also ensures that every one concerned has the same information.

Advantages

- It serves as evidence of events and proceedings.
- It provides a permanency of record for future references.
- It reduces the possibility of misunderstandings and misinterpretations.
- It can save time when many persons must be contacted at the same time.
- It is reliable for transmitting lengthy statistical data.
- It appears formal and authoritative for action.
- It can be checked for accuracy, which may not be always possible in verbal communication.

Disadvantages

- It can be very time consuming for lengthy reports.
- There is no feedback opportunity to be sure that the receiver has understood the message.
- Written material may leak out before time, causing disruption in its effectiveness.

- It leads to excessive formality in personal relations.

3.4 Ambiguity Avoidance

As a manager (concerned with getting things done) your view of words should be pragmatic rather than philosophical. Thus, words mean not what the dictionary says they do but rather what the speaker intended.

Suppose your manager gives you an instruction, which contains an ambiguity, which neither of you notice and which results in you producing entirely the wrong product? Who is at fault? The answer must be: who cares? Your time has been wasted, the needed product is delayed (or lead); attributing blame may be satisfying (or defensive) exercise but it does not address the problem. In everything you say or hear, you must look out for possible misunderstanding and clarify the ambiguity.

A second problem is that some people simply make mistakes. Your job is not simply to spot ambiguities but also to counter inconsistencies. Thus, if I now advocate that the wise manager should seek out (perhaps humorous) books on entomology you would deduce that the word should have been etymology. More usual, however, is that in thinking over several alternatives you may suffer a momentary confusion and say one of them while meaning another. There are good scientific reasons why this happens, you have to be aware of the potential problem and counter for it.

The word has multiple meanings, it might not be the one intended, and you may have misheard it in the first place - how do you know what the speaker meant?

Rule 1: Play Back for Confirmation

Simple, you ask for confirmation. You say "let me see if I have understood correctly", you are saying that "and you rephrase what the speaker said." If this "play black" version is acknowledged as being correct by the original speaker, then you have a greater degree of confidence in you. For any view point/message/decision, there should be a clear, concise and verified statement of what was said; without this someone will get it wrong.

Rule 2: Write Back for Confidence

But do not stop there. If your time and effort depend upon it, you should write it down and send it, to everyone involved as a double check. This has several advantages:

- Further clarification: is this what you thought we agreed?
- Consistency check-the act of writing may highlight defects, omissions.
- A formal stage: a statement of the accepted position provides a springboard from which to proceed.
- Evidence: hindsight often blurs previous ignorance and people often fail to recall their previous errors.

Rule 3: Give Background for Context

When speaking yourself, you can often counter for possible problems by adding information, and so providing a broader context in which your words can be understood. Thus, there is less scope for alternative interpretations since fewer are consistent. When others are speaking, you should deliberately ask questions yourself to establish and context in which they are thinking.

Practical Points

As with all effective communications, you should decide (in advance) on the purpose of the conversation and the plan for achieving it. There is no alternative to this. Therefore, one should have clear understanding of the context and his own goals. You have to plan. The following are a few techniques to help the conversation along.

Assertiveness - The definition of to assert is: "to declare; state clearly". This is your aim. If someone argues against you, even loses temper, you should be quietly assertive. Much has been written to preach this simple fact and commonly the final message is a three-fold plan of action.

- Acknowledge what is being said by showing an understanding of the position, or by simply replaying it (a polite way of saying "I heard you already").

- State your own point of view clearly and concisely with perhaps a little supporting evidence.

- State what you want to happen next (move it forward).

Thus we have something like: yes, I see why you need the report by tomorrow; however, I have no time today to prepare the document because I am in a meeting with a customer this afternoon; either one could give you the raw data and you could work on it yourself.

You will have to make many personal judgment calls when being assertive. There will certainly be times when a bit of quiet force from you will win the day but there will be times when this will get nowhere, particularly with more senior (and unenlightened) management. In the latter case, you must agree to abide by the decision of the senior manager but you should make your objection (and reasons) clearly known. For yourself, always that your subordinates might be right when they disagree with you and if events prove them so, acknowledge that fact gracefully.

Confrontations - When you have a difficult encounter, be professional; do not lose your self-control because, simply, it is of no use. Some managers believe that it is useful for "discipline" to keep staff a little nervous. Thus, these managers are slightly volatile and will be willing "to let them have it" when the situation demands. If you do this, you must be consistent and fair so that your staff know where they stand. If you deliberately loose your temper for effect, then that is your decision - however, you must never lose control.

Insults are ineffective – If you call people names, then they are unlikely to actually listen to what you have to say; in the short term you may feel some relief at "getting it off your chest", but in the long run you are merely perpetuating the problem since you are not addressing it. This is common sense. There are two implications Firstly, even under pressure, you have to remember this. Secondly, what you consider fair comment may be insulting to another and the same problem emerges. Before you say anything, stop, establish what you want as the outcome, plan how to achieve this, and then speak.

Finally, if you are going to criticise or discipline someone, always assume that you have misunderstood the situation and ask questions first which check the facts. This simple courtesy will save you from much embarrassment.

Seeking information – There are two ways of phrasing any question: one way (the closed question) is likely to lead to a simple grunt in reply (yes, no, maybe), the second way (the open question) will hand over the speaking role to someone else and force them to say something a little more informative. Open questions are extremely easy to formulate you establish in your own mind the topic aim of the question and then you start the sentence with the words: WHAT - WHEN - WHICH - WHY - WHERE – HOW.

Let others speak – Of course, there is more to a conversation (managed or otherwise) than the flow of information. You may also have to win that information by winning the attention and confidence of the other person. There are many forms of flattery - the most effective is to give people your interest. To get Indira to give you all her knowledge, you must give her all your attention; talk to her about her view on the subject. Ask questions: what do you think about that idea, have you ever met this problem before, how would you tackle this situation? Silence is effective - and much under-used. People are nervous of silence and try to fill it. You can use this if you are seeking information. You ask the question, you lean back, the person answers, you nod and smile, you keep quiet, and the person continues with more detail simply to fill your silence.

3.5 Public Speaking

A manager's work will involve oral as well as written communication. Probably the written communication will give more problems. But the oral communication takes up more time. In fact, a manager is likely to spend more time in oral communication than in any other work activity.

Much of the oral communication that goes on in organisation is informal. Primarily, it is the face-to-face communication that takes place whenever people get together. Obviously, this is a form of communication in which we all have experience. And most of us do a reasonably good job of it.

In addition to the informal talking that goes on in organisation, various kinds of more formal oral communication takes place. Sometimes people must make formal presentations, speeches, lectures, oral reports, etc. Sometimes they conduct and participate in committee meetings, conferences and group discussions. From time to time, they have oral interviews with job applicants, departing workers and employees. Even when they write letters and reports, they often bring these messages orally as spoken dictation. All these more formal kinds of oral communication are a part of the work.

The most difficult kind of oral communication for most people is a formal speech. Most of us feel uncomfortable speaking before others and generally do a poor job of it. But it need not be this way. With efforts we can improve our speaking. We can do this by first learning good speaking techniques. Then we put these techniques into practice.

Your first step in formal speech making is to determine the topic of your presentation. In some cases, you will be assigned a topic, usually one within your area of specialisation. In fact, when you are asked to make a speech on a specified topic, it is likely to be because of your knowledge of it. If you are not assigned a topic, you must find one on your search for a suitable topic, you will do well to be guided by three basic factors. The first is your own background and knowledge. Any topic you select should be one with which you are comfortable - one within your areas of proficiency. The second is the interest of your audience. Selecting something your audience can appreciate and understand is vital to the success of your speech. The third is the occasion of the speech. Whatever you select should fit the occasion.

After you have determined what to talk about, you should gather the information that will form the basis of your speech. In some cases, this involves searching through your mind for supporting experience or perhaps for idea development. Sometimes you will need to conduct primary research in a library. With some topics, you may need to consult colleagues or people from other organisation. In short, you do whatever is necessary to get the information that will form the basis of your presentation.

When you have all the information you need, you are ready to begin organising your speech. Although variations are sometimes appropriate, usually you should follow the time honoured order of a speech: introduction, body, and conclusion - the same indirect order used in some reports.

Although not really a part of the speech, the first words usually spoken are the getting. Your getting of course, should fit the audience. "Ladies and Gentlemen" is appropriate for a mixed audience: "Gentlemen" fits an all male audience : of some speakers eliminate the getting and begin directly with the speech, especially in more informal and technical presentations.

The introduction of a speech has much to same goal as the introduction of a written report : to prepare the listener (or reader) to receive the message. But the introduction of a speech usually has the additional requirement of arousing interest. Unless you can arouse interest at the beginning, your presentation is likely to fail.

The techniques of attracting interest are limited only by the imagination. In some cases, beginning with a human-interest story may be successful, for story telling has strong appeal. Humour is another possibility and is probably the most widely used technique. Yet another technique is the startling statement - presenting facts and ideas that awake the mind. Whatever you choose should meet the additional requirement : It should lead to, or set the theme of the speech. In other words, there should be a close tie-in between the opening interest gaining remarks and the subject of the speech.

Following the interest-gaining opening, it is appropriate to state the subject (theme) of your speech. In fact, when your audience already is interested in what you have to say, you can begin here and skip the attention-gaining opening. Presentation of technical topics to technical audiences typically begins this way. Whether you lead to a statement of your topic or begin with it, your statement should be clear and complete.

Sometimes you may find it undesirable to reveal a position early because of the nature of your subject. In these cases, you may prefer to move in to your subject indirectly - to build up your case before revealing your position. You should use this inductive pattern especially when your goal is to persuade - when you need to move your audience's views from one position to another.

Organising the body of your speech is much like organising the body of a report. You take the whole and decide it into comparable parts. Then you take these parts and decide them. You continue to divide as far as it is practical to do so. In speeches, however, you are more likely to use factors as the basis of division than time, place or quantity. The reason is that in most speeches your presentation is likely to build around issues and questions that are subtopics of the subject. These issues and questions, of course, are factors.

Like most reports the speech usually ends with a conclusion, here you bring all that you have presented to a head. You achieve the speech's goal. In doing this, you should consider including these three elements in your close: *(i)* A restatement of your subject, *(ii)* A summary of the key points developed in the presentation, and *(iii)* A statement of the conclusion for main message. Usually it is effective to bring the speech to a climactic close, i.e. make it the high point of the speech. You can do this by presenting the concluding message in strong language. In words, that will gain attention and be remembered.

3.5.1 Creating an Effective Speech

The speakers are essentially a part of the message. Your audience takes in not only the words you communicate but also what they see in you. And what they see in you can significantly affect the meanings that develop in their minds. Thus, you should careful evaluate your personal effect on the message you present you should do whatsoever you can to detect and overcome shortcomings and to sharpen any strengths. The seven important steps to create an effective speech are:

The first step in making a speech is choosing a topic. We will assume you already have a topic since your qualifications, the audience, or the occasion usually determines it. If you do not have a topic, your most effective speeches will come from a topic you are familiar with or that you want to learn more about.

The second step is to define the purpose of your speech. Are you speaking to convince your audience, inform your audience, or a combination of the two? And, what are you persuading your audience to do, or what are you informing them about? The answers to these questions will define the purpose of your speech.

The third step is to get to know your audience. Get to know the demographic features of your audience. You want to know how large the audience will be, what sort of setting or conditions you will be speaking in, how the audience feels about the topic, and how the audience feels about you as the speaker. Gauge how important these factors will be on the speaking situation and adjust your speech accordingly. Keep in mind the audience is the focus of your speech, and you are looking for a positive response from them.

The fourth step is to gather information for your speech. There are countless sources of information, but here are a few : interviews, the Internet, scholarly journals, government documents, newspapers, and magazines. This information can be used in your speech in a variety of ways. It may be used to supply examples for supporting your ideas, or as statistics to quantify your ideas.

The fifth step is to organise your speech. Start by identifying the main points you want to make, and then put them in an order that makes sense to your topic. You can order them chronologically if your topic covers a sequence of events; specially if you are describing something from top to bottom, east to west, or according to some other avenue; or, problem-solution order if you are presenting a problem followed by a solution.

The sixth step is adding an introduction to your speech. The introduction is aimed at getting the attention of your audience. There are several ways to accomplish this, the most common are: relating the topic to the audience, shocking the audience with an intriguing or astonishing statement, questioning the audience, or telling a suspenseful or provocative story. The next phases of the introduction are to state the topic of your speech so the audience will know what you are going to talk about, and to preview the main points of your speech so the audience will know what to listen for.

The seventh step is adding a conclusion to your speech. First, signal to the audience that your speech is coming to a close by using phrases such as "In conclusion," "In closing," and "Let me end by saying." Second, reinforce the main point of your speech. You can do this by simply restating your main points, ending with a quotation that summarises your main points, or by making a dramatic statement that emphasises your main points.

Confidence

A primary characteristic of effective oral reporting is confidence. This includes your confidence in yourself and your audience's confidence in you. Actually, the two are complementary, for your confidence in yourself tends to produce an image that gives your audience confidence in you. Similarly, your audience's confidence in you can give you a sense of security, thereby making you more confident of your ability.

You can prepare your presentation attentively and practice it thoroughly. Such careful preliminary work will give you confidence in yourself. Having confidence leads to more effective communication, which in turn builds confidence in your listener's mind. Another thing you can do to gain confidence is checking your physical appearance carefully. Unfair and illogical as it may be, certain styles of dress and hair create strong images in people's minds. Thus, if you want to communicate effectively, you should analyse the audience you seek to reach. You should work to develop the physical appearance that will project an image in which your audience can have confidence. Yet another suggestion is simply to talk in strong, clear tones. Such tones do much to project an image of confidence.

Sincerity

Your listeners will be quick to detect insincerity in you. When they do, they are likely to give little weight to what you say. On the other hand, sincerity is a valuable aid to conviction especially if the audience has confidence in your ability. What you can do to project an image of sincerity is clear: You must be sincere. Pretending of sincerity rarely succeeds.

Thoroughness

Thoroughness in your presentation generally will make your message better received than skimpy or hurried coverage. Thorough coverage gives the impression that you have taken time and care, such an impression tends to make the message believable. But you can overdo thoroughness. If you present the information in too much detail, your listeners may become lost in a sea of information. The secret is to select the important information and leave out the unimportant. Selecting the important information, of course, requires that you use good judgement.

Friendliness

A speaker who projects an image of friendliness has a significant advantage in communicating. People simply like people who are friendly and are more receptive to what they say. Like sincerity, friendliness is difficult to pretend. It must be honest, if it is to be effective. But with most people friendliness is honest, for most people want to be friendly. Some just are unable to project the desired friendly image. With a little self-diagnosis and some mirror watching or videotaping as you practice speaking, you can find ways to improve the friendliness of your image that shall further enhance your speaking image.

3.6 Making Presentations

We spend an incredible amount of time during our professional and personal lives, "Making presentations" and "Listening to presentations". Most of our presentations are informal, with family and friends, we regularly try to inform, convince, reject, query, questions and solicit opinions. At times our PRESENTATIONS reflect every day activity, routine and largely uneventful. At other times, our presentations reflect strong opinions, needs and feelings.

As we move up the ladder of professional responsibility, more and more of our time is spent in MAKING PRESENTATIONS, both formal and informal, to peers; and superiors.

- Do we question our ability as presenters?
- Do we look for the concrete ways to increase power and force-fullness of our PRESENTATIONS?
- Do we try to present an issue or idea with exceptional effectiveness?

Effective presentation skills are one of the most important talents that a professional in any field can muster. The ability to make an effective presentation increases with PRACTICE, PRACTICE and MORE PRACTICE.

3.6.1 Model for Developing Presentation Outline

A simple and easy to use model for developing your presentation outline may be:

I. Introduce the topic

II. State the key issues
Issue (i) - Sub-points and examples.
Issue (ii) - Sub-points and examples.
Issue (iii) - Sub-points and examples.

III. Conclude summaries by restating issues.

The introduction - This element of your presentation is vital for a number of reasons since it is where you make your first impression. If the beginning of your presentation is weak, you may never get a chance to recover; instead, your audience will turn off, hearing very little of what you have to say. The listeners rapidly take into account, either consciously or sub-consciously when watching your presentation the followings as to :

- What you say.
- How you look.
- And how you sound.

Good Introductions achieve the following objectives; they are :

- Get your audience attention.
- Identify the topic's.
- Establish the importance of the topic to the audience.
- Preview the main thrust of your presentation.

The importance of presentations may be established by including one or two "ATTENTION GRABBERS". Attention grabbers are techniques for heightening audience interest. Start your listeners with striking or shocking statements. Telling a story is another way to introduce your topic and put your audience into the presentation. The first three minutes of your presentations are critical, so be sure to identify your topic, establish the importance of the subject and focus on something that is easy for you to talk about.

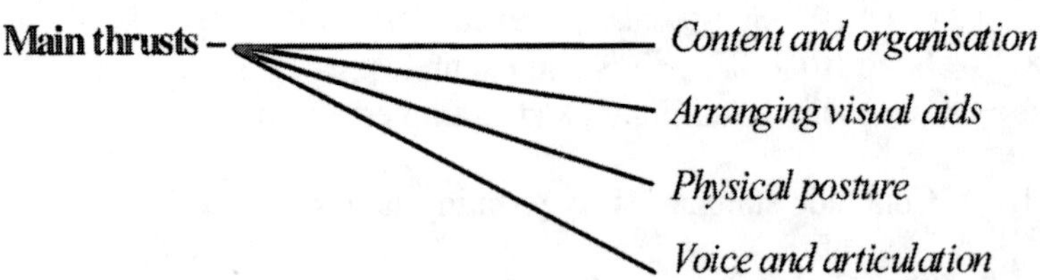

In terms of CONTENT AND ORGANISATION, it is important to be able to organise and group your information in such a way that your audience finds it interesting, informative and memorable.

Using VISUAL AIDS are, excellent techniques for affecting the way in which your audience interprets your presentation. Charts, overheads, photographs and whiteboards are key devices, which are easily used to distinguish and emphasise your message and skills. One picture is worth a thousand words or so the saying goes.

Your audience continually interprets your PHYSICAL POSTURE, dress, body movement, body language and gestures. Keep in mind, the audience see you before they hear you, so you can be sure that the audience has already drawn certain conclusions before you get a chance to open your mouth?

"EYES" are particularly important. Everyone watching you will interpret how you use your eyes to make contact with the audience under different conditions.

Finally your VOICE AND ARTICULATION is critical element of a successful presentation.

- Can you be heard and understood by everyone in the room? - THE VOLUME
- Is your word choice appropriate for the occasions? - THE LANGUAGE
- Do you speak too fast, too slow, too high or too low? - PITCH AND INFLECTION
- Do you pronounce every word fully and accurately? - PRONUNCIATION
- Are you nervous?
- Can the audience hear your nervousness?

Critique and feedback are critical for everyone who wants to know what his presentation strengths and weaknesses are.

Conclude or the ending – The ending is your last chance to impress the audience which should be brief and to the point. Many good presentations suffer from long-winded summaries that undo the point or worse yet add-ons that detract from the core theme. The ending should be signaled to the audience. Ending with a quotation is a good touch. Another option is to make a dramatic statement. Recapping the key elements in your presentation is critical in order to reinforce your message. A simple formula for a good ending may include the following: Tell them what you told them (Not more than three sentences). Thank the audience and compliment them. End with a short quote. In your conclusion make sure you summarise your message in a concise, convincing manner.

3.6.2 Oral Reporting

A special form of speech is the oral report. You are more likely to make oral reports than speeches in business, and the oral reports you make are likely to be important. Unfortunately, most of us have had little experience and even less instruction in oral reporting. In its broadest sense, an oral report is any presentation of factual information using the spoken word. An oral report logically limits coverage to factual information. By this definition, an oral report covers much of the information exchanged in the daily conduct of business. It varies widely in formality. At one extreme, it covers the most routine and informal reporting situations. At the other, it includes highly formal presentations. Because the more informal exchanges are little more than routine conversations, clearly, these are the reports, requiring the most care and skill. Oral reports are much like written reports. The first major difference between oral and written reports is that the latter permits greater use of visual aids to communication.

Planning the Oral Report

For short, informal reports, of course, planning may be minimal. But for more formal presentations, particularly those involving audiences of more than one, proper planning is likely to be as involved as that for a comparable written report.

Determination of Report Objective

Your first step in planning an oral report is to determine your objective. In this step you should state the report goal in clear, concise language just as you would for a written report.

Then you should clearly state the factors involved in achieving this goal. These steps will guide you to the information you must gather and to the framework around which to build your presentation.

In the process of determining your goal, you must be aware of your general objective - that is, you must decide on your general purpose in making the presentation. Is it to persuade? To inform? To recommend? Your decision here will have a major influence on your development of the material for presentation and perhaps even on the presentation itself.

Organisation of Content

Even so, the same information presented orally and in writing is not necessarily presented in the same way. Time pressure, for example, may justify direct presentation for an oral report. The same report problem presented in writing might be best arranged in the indirect order. A reader in a hurry can always pass over to the report's conclusion or ending. The listener does not have this option.

Although oral reports may use either the direct or indirect order, the indirect is by far the more widely used as well as the more logical. Because your audience is unlikely to know the problem well, you will need some introductory comments to prepare them to receive the message. You may also need introductory words to arouse interest, stimulate curiosity, or impress the audience with the subjects' importance. The main goal of the introductory remarks is to state the purpose, define unfamiliar terms, explain limitations, describe scope, and generally cover all the necessary introductory subjects.

In the body of the oral report, you should develop the goals you have set. Here too there is much similarity with the written report. Division of subject matter into comparable parts, logical order, introductory paragraphs, concluding paragraphs, and such are equally important with both forms.

The oral report is likely to have a final summary tacked on regardless of whether it has a conclusion or recommendation. In a sense, this final summary serves the purpose of an executive summary by bringing together all the really important information, analysis, conclusions and recommendations in the report. It also serves to assist the memory by placing added emphasis on the points that should stand out.

3.6.3 Improving Presentation Skill

Making effective presentations to groups or key individuals is part of any executive's job. Delivering a clearly understandable message that gains the support of the listeners obviously requires expertise in public speaking. You need to make an effort to understand the perspective of your audience so that you can adjust your presentation based on feedback during or after the session. Public speaking ranks highest on the list of situations people fear most (followed by death!) Overcoming this fear requires education and practice, practice, practice! Few of us are born to be excellent public speakers. We offer encouragement to those who feel insecure — don't give up! Many organisations offer proven techniques for overcoming fear and assistance in mastering master speaking skills. We have seen many; many people become accomplished speakers, who in the past became speechless when asked to speak in public. Some tips for improving presentation skills:

1. Know your subject! This is most important.

2. Prepare for the speaking situation (outline, writing the entire presentation, delivering it to friends or whatever works for you). Even professional public speakers take time to prepare themselves.

3. Prepare outlines and overheads to help develop your confidence in your presentation (part of knowing your topic well).

4. Have your outline (or overheads, slides or note cards) with you to refer to as you make the presentation and to trigger your thoughts as you speak.

5. In the early stages of your preparation, ask someone you trust to listen to your presentation and give you honest

feedback in a one-on-one situation. Ask them what works well and what needs improvement. The more important the results of your presentation are to you, the more important it is to get help in refining your presentation.

6. Take classes where you are able to develop presentations and have them critiqued (e.g., classes in public speaking or verbal presentation skills, Toastmasters).

7. Tape your presentation (videotape is best) and ask others to criticise your presentation. Watch yourself and learn to look for subtle body language clues to your confidence or insecurity.

8. Talk to people you respect about how they learned to speak well. Ask them to coach you (if that is appropriate) or try to find someone you admire who will work with you.

9. When you are confident, relaxed and enthusiastic about your topic, that comes through strongly to your audience. Remember how much comes through non-verbal clues.

10. Ask for feedback from your audience about your presentation and pay attention to what they say.

11. In workshops, ask the participants to introduce themselves, state why they are there and what they hope to gain from the presentation. (This is most appropriate if you are making a speech or giving a class to strangers). Based on the participants' needs and expectations, you may adjust your presentation as you go through it.

12. In a management presentation especially (e.g., to present your new budget or present sales information), stop occasionally to ask if people understand what you have said.

13. If you have an executive coach (or someone who can play that role), have them sit in on your presentations and help you pick up clues from the group. (We did this very effectively with one of our clients who had been promoted to department

manager. We used hand signals and other cues to let her know when she was going too fast, too slow or missing the body language of an executive group where she gave regular presentations).

14. And, most of all—Practice, practice, practice!

3.7 Dictating Letters and Reports

When you advance to an executive position, dictating is likely to be one of your major communication activities. The odds are that you will dictate most of your letters. You may even dictate reports - especially shorter, more informal ones. Thus, professional executives may adopt the following techniques and procedures of dictating:

Gather the Facts: Your first logical step in dictating is to get all the information you need for the message. This step involves such activities as getting past correspondence from files, consulting with other employees about the situation, and determining organisation policy. The important point is to get everything you need so that you can work without interruption.

Plan the Message: With the facts of the case before you, you next plan the message. You may prefer to do this step in your mind. Or you may prefer to nail down a few notes or an outiine. Whatever your preference, your goal in this step is to decide what your message will be and how you will present it.

Give Preliminary Information and Instructions: Your first step in the actual process of dictating is to give the stenographers specific instructions. Included here are instructions about special handling, enclosures, forms, and page layout. Also included is all the additional information about the message, such as mailing address, subject line, attention line, and salutation.

Make the Words Flow: Your next step is to talk through the message. As simple as this sounds, you are likely to have problems doing it. Thinking out loud to a stenographer or a dictating machine frightens most of us at first the result is likely to be slow and awkward dictation. Overcoming this problem requires self-discipline. You should force yourself to concentrate and make the words flow. Your goal should be to get the words out - to talk through the message

Speak in Strong, Clear Voice: Because your dictation must be heard, you should dictate in a strong, clear voice. You should speak slowly enough to clearly separate the words. Words that do not stand out clearly can cause delays in work as well as errors in the message.

Give Paragraphing, Punctuation, and Other Mechanics as Needed: If your stenographer is competent in writing correctness and form, you may leave this matter to him or her. On most occasions, however, you are wise, to dictate most such information.

Avoid Using Asides: Asides (side comments not intended to be part of the message) are better not used. They tend to confuse the stenographer, who must determine which words are part of the message and which are not.

Read Back Intelligently: Although you should try to talk through the message without interruption, sometimes you will need to stop and get a read-back of what you have dictated. But do this only when necessary. More than likely, a read back result from confused thinking. You will find read-back especially helpful at the end of the message for giving you a check on the overall effect of your words.

3.8 Using the Telephone

Yet another communication activity in which you are likely to engage heavily is telephoning. Perhaps your first thought is that a discussion of this activity is unimportant. After all, most of us have had long experience using the telephone and may feel we have little to learn about it. No doubt, some of us have excellent telephone skills. But you have only to make calls to a few randomly selected businesses to learn that not all telephone users are proficient. You will encounter some bad-tempered, cold greetings and a variety of discourtesies. You will also find some instances of inefficient use of time (which, of course, is costly).

At the beginning of a telephone conversation that you have initiated, it is good practice to state the purpose of the call. Then you should systematically cover all the points involved. You should plan really important calls, even perhaps making notes of the points to cover. Then you should follow your notes to make certain you cover all points.

Courteous procedure during a telephone conversation is much the same as in face-to-face conversation. You listen when the other person is talking. You refrain from interrupting. You avoid dominating the conversation. Perhaps most important of all, you cover your message quickly, saving time (and money) for all concerned.

3.8.1 Need for Favourable Voice Quality

In reviewing good telephone techniques, keep in mind that a telephone conversation is a unique form of oral communication. Only voices are heard; the speakers are not seen. The only impressions received are from the words and the quality of the voices. Thus, it is extremely important that when speaking by telephone you work to make your voice sound cheerful and friendly.

One often suggested way to improve your telephone voice is to talk as if you are face to face with the other person - even smiling and gesturing as you talk, if this helps you to be more natural. In addition, you would do well to put into practice concerning use of voice in speaking (voice quality, variation in pitch and speed). Perhaps the best instructional device for this problem is to tape record one of your telephone conversations. Then judge for yourself how you come across and what you must do to improve.

3.8.2 Aspects of Telephone Etiquette

There are seven different aspects of telephone etiquette to consider.

1. General Telephone Etiquette

- Identify yourself, with your first and last name, when answering the phone.
- Return phones calls within 24 hours, and apologise if the call is late.

- Identify yourself when you place a call. Say your name, the company, business or department you represent. Then state the nature of your call. If you do not identify yourself, expect to be asked and do not take offense.

2. Interoffice Phone Etiquette

- Don't hover outside a coworker's office or cubicle waiting for him or her to finish up a phone call.

- Leave, and try again later.

- Don't listen in on coworkers' phone conversations. If you share office space with someone, this may be unavoidable, but try to keep busy while the person is talking – and never comment on what you've just overheard!

3. Voice Mail

- Outgoing messages should include your name and company name. If applicable, mention the job you handle to prevent having to route the message to someone else.

- Let the caller know how to reach a live person in an emergency.

- Keep your outgoing message current. If you're going to be out of the office, your message should say so. When you go away, state the date you'll be back and whether or not you'll be calling in for messages, or whom to contact in your absence.

4. Call-Waiting

Unless you are expecting an urgent call and say so, it's impolite to continually put the person to whom you're speaking on hold while you take another call. Say, "I have another call, can you hold just a second?" Take the other call, explain you're on another line and will call back shortly. Then quickly return to your first caller.

5. Speakerphones

Although a speakerphone is a great convenience when several people need to participate in a conference call, in a two-person conversation, it often annoys or offends the person whose voice is broadcast. Use it sparingly, and always tell the person on the other end that a speakerphone is being used. Try to avoid using it with a client.

6. Cellular Phones

- Try to remove yourself from a public area to a quiet corner of the room so as not to bother others.

- If you must make or take a call, keep it short and as discrete as possible.

7. Placing Someone on Hold

- Make sure it's for a good reason, such as pulling the person's file or answering another line.

- Ask the person if he or she will hold, and wait for a response rather than assuming the answer is yes.

- Never keep a caller on hold for more than a minute. If you have to take longer than that, return to the person and tell them that you absolute have to take a few minutes longer, and ask if she wouldn't prefer that you call her back.

- When you return to the caller, thank them for holding.

3.9 Interviews, Negotiations and Reflections

Another communication activity in which you are likely to heavily participate is interviewing. You will probably participate in a number of forms of interviewing. The employment interview is one - perhaps the first interview you will experience in business. But after you have begun work, there will be others. One possibility is the interview done in the periodic evaluations some companies make of their workers. Primarily these interviews are a means of communicating the evaluations. Another possibility is the exit interview. When workers leave a company, they may be interviewed to determine their reasons for leaving. Then there are the interviews conducted by company personnel to gather information on such matters as worker's attitudes, working conditions, managerial effectiveness, and worker plans.

Because interviewing is a form of personal communication, Usually between two people, it is not a precise activity; that is, there are no hard and fast rules to follow. Instead, interviewing is a flexible activity that must follow the good judgment of the people involved, nevertheless, well-established guidelines exit.

3.9.1 Conducting Interviews

Because the interviewer is in charge, the interviews success is in his or her hands. Thus, it is especially important that the interviewer knows and follows these general guidelines.

Plan the Interview: You conduct most interviews because you need information. Thus as a starting point you should determine what information you need. Usually you can write your needs in a series of specific questions. You should make such a list and use it as the outline for the interview.

Put the Interviewee at Ease: Chances are that the interviewee will be nervous. Because nervous people are not good subjects for interviewing, you should try to put the interviewee at ease. How you should do this varies with the person involved and with your social skills. You could, for example, begin with some friendly talk on a point of common interest. You could begin with comments or questions about the interviewee-hometown, sports interests, hobbies, and the like.

Make the Purpose Clear: Your interviewee should know the purpose of the interview from the beginning. Of course, sometimes the interviewee knows simply from the nature of the interview, as in an employment situation. But if he or she does not know, you should explain the purpose clearly and honestly.

Let the Interviewee Do Most of the Talking: You can get the information you seek only when the interviewee talks. Thus, you should let the interviewee do most of the talking. You should talk only to guide the course of the interviewee - to carry the discussion through the specific questions you want to cover. Because some interviewees are reluctant to talk, you may need to work to get them to participate. But you should never attempt to put words in their mouths; rather, you should try to put them at ease and get them into an informal, relaxed mood.

Guide the Interview: Although the interviewee does the talking, your task is to guide the interview through the information needed that is to follow the plan you set up in the beginning. You ask specific questions, and you end answers when you have the information you need. In guiding the interview, you will need to handle moments of silence. Brief periods of silence may be all right, for sometimes they lead to additional information but too much silence can be awkward for all concerned.

Listen: You should listen carefully to all that the interviewee says. The purpose of an interview is to get certain information by listening. In addition to listening, you should give the appearance of listening. Your interviewee will be more relaxed and talk more if they feel they have your undivided attention.

Keep a Record: As you conduct interviews to get information, you will need to make a record of the information. How you record information may vary with the situation. When you need much detailed information, you may need to take notes during the interview. Because your writing may be disturbing to the interviewee, at the beginning of the interview you should explain why you must take notes. Even after explaining, you should write as quickly and unobtrusively as possible. When you can remember the information you seek after the interview, you need not write during it. But you should record the information soon after the interview is over. As you know, few of us can remember such information for very long.

End the Interview: Because you are in charge of the interview, you are the one who should end it. If the situation justifies it, some friendly talk can follow the questioning. But you should avoid letting the conversation trail off to meaningless talk. One good way to end an interview is to ask a finalising type question-one that indicates that the interview is over. This one does the job well: Is there anything else you would like to tell me? (Pause) if not, thanks for giving me your time.

3.9.2 Preparing for the Interviews

When you are the one being interviewed, you have little control over the situation. Nevertheless, you can help make the interview successful. The following guidelines tell you how.

Prepare for the Interview: When you know the nature of the interview, you should prepare for it. Your preparation should consist mainly of anticipating the questions you are likely to be asked and forming answers to them. It also may include gathering additional information. In a job interview, for example, you would be wise to learn what you can about the organisations - its history, what it does, its plan, its current activities. By showing your knowledge during the interview, you can impress the interviewer. With your interest, even if you prepare diligently, however, you are unlikely to cover all that will be asked. So be prepared for the unexpected. Make an appropriate appearance: What the interviewer sees is a part of the message received. Thus, you should do what you can to make an appropriate appearance. What is appropriate varies with the situation. In most cases, you will find the conventional standards of neatness and dress to be desirable. In addition, you will want your posture, facial expressions, and bodily movements to give favourable impressions. You will especially want to avoid appearing nervous.

Show Interest: You can improve the impressions you make in most interview situations by showing interest. How you should show interest varies with the occasion. But you will always help your case by looking at the interviewer and giving her or him your undivided attention.

Answer Correctly and Completely: If the interview serves a good purpose, it deserves correct and complete answers. You should give them.

Practice Courtesy: Probably you know very well the value of courtesy. You know that it is a major part of the impression you make in every human contact. The interview is no exception.

3.10 Written Communication and Written Communication Modes

3.10.1 Memos

Writing memos as well as novels helps us come to know what we really think. Writing is a rigorous discipline that demands a greater precision of thought than speech. Why? Memos by design do not encourage clear and timely feedback. The difficulty occurs when readers fail to understand the memo or, more seriously, fail to recognise that they do not understand. Thus, the major responsibility for communication lays with the writer, but writer plagues many who lack necessary skills their clarity and brevity.

Training can help : One exemplary study showed that using a "high-impact" memo style, which included starting the objective in the first paragraph, bold type headings, active verbs and simple sentences was more effective than the typical "bureaucratic" style that included abstract language, passive verbs, no personal pronouns, and the purpose statement in the last paragraph. The high impact style took about 20 per cent less time to read, was more effectively comprehended, and did not need to be re-reading as often as the bureaucratic style. Surprisingly, the "bureaucratic" writer was seen as more "dynamic and forceful". One explanation offered was that the bureaucratic styles fits more closely with the organisation's culture by allowing the writer coverage of his "vital assets" too. Thus, revising writing styles in an organisation also may involve changing the corporate culture.

The predominant attribute of an inter-office memo, like all written mediums, is that it provides a permanent record of communication that is useful for documentation purposes. Consequently, a memo imbues a sense of formality. Also, by its very nature, a memo allows the receiver to control the time of consumption, which frees the written medium from the normal space-time constraints of oral channels. Readers have something concrete to refer back to at their leisure. Announcing routine organisational changes, transmitting information between geographically separated divisions, or reporting meeting schedules and agendas are examples of how the positive characteristics of memos can be fully utilised. Yet memos carry a sense of finality about communication that may give senders a false sense of security about their effectiveness.

3.10.2 Reports

A report is an account of a particular activity, incorporating the results of observations, experiments and analysis. In most cases, they summarise information and offer recommendations. Short reports, those with five or fewer pages, are often presented in letter or even memo format. Longer reports are more formal in nature, and typically include a title page and executive summary. The number and type of sections in a report can vary enormously, depending on the content, presentation style and preferences of the reader and audience. However, most reports include the following:

(A) Description of the Problem or Issue being Addressed

The report begins with a section that describes the problem or issue being discussed in order to clarify and confirm the topic for the reader. This is done at the beginning of the report so that there will be no confusion, for the reader, regarding the topic and purpose. This section of the report need not be long. In fact, two or three sentences may be enough, though a longer description may be required if the issue is complex or multifaceted.

(B) Overview and Background Informations

The second section, the overview and background information, should be detailed enough to ensure the reader will understand why the issue is being examined; who or what motivated the examination, and the major elements that form the basis for the evaluation and report. Although some readers may find this section of the report to be repetitive, particularly if they are familiar with the issue, this section describes the writer's perspective and the biases he/she brings to the study, both by including certain information and by excluding some.

(C) Body of the Report

The third section contains the body of the report. This is the description of the data, observations, experiments and findings. It is important that this section of the report demonstrate a balanced perspective. Both advantages and disadvantages should be included. The length of this section of the report will vary. However, keep in mind that a longer report will have fewer readers than a shorter report, and one of the purposes of a report is to condense information.

(D) Conclusions and Recommendations

The final section of the report summarises, draws conclusions and makes recommendations. It is important that this section flows naturally from the data, and that the information in the preceding section supports the conclusions. By the time a reader reaches the section on recommendations, he should not be in doubt the conclusion that will be drawn. Longer reports, those with more than four or five pages, will include an executive summary. This is placed at the beginning of the report. The length of the executive summary will depend on the length and complexity of the report. For a report of six or seven pages, an executive summary of three paragraphs will be sufficient. If the report is forty pages in length, the executive summary might include one sentence stating the purpose of the report, two or three sentences justifying the study or describing why it was completed, an overview of the major findings, and a brief description of the recommendations and supporting rationale. The purpose of the executive summary is twofold.

- First, it provides the reader who doesn't have the time (or inclination) to read the entire report with a snapshot of the major points.

- Second, for the audience that will read the entire paper. It prepares them to appreciate your method and builds support for your conclusions.

The order of presentation in the body of a report can vary, depending on your personal preference, the points you are trying to make, and your audience. A standard approach is to use a chronological order. With this approach, you describe the events, studies and observations in the order they happened. In many cases this is the easiest approach for your audience to understand. With the chronological approach, the report can be written in such a way that your readers will understand with complications or surprises you faced because they will be experiencing the data sequentially, the way you experienced it.

Deciding to write a report in chronological order requires making a decision with regard to where or at what point in time you will begin the report. This decision should be based on the needs of your readers. Remember, the reader does not want to know everything you know, just the key points that will permit an informed understanding leading to the best decisions. The second issue, the level of detail in a chronological report, should be dealt with in the same manner.

A different approach to report writing is the order of importance or magnitude of the event style. In this format the writer presents the data according to its relative importance. The most important elements or the most pressing issues are dealt with first. This is a good approach if you don't expect your audience to read the entire report, or if you believe their level of interest will taper off as they read the report. The earlier points generate most of the attention, as befits their importance. The problem with this approach is that, by definition, the report becomes less interesting as it develops. Therefore, even interested readers may be encouraged to browse rather than read the later sections.

A probable approach is the problem solving order. With this technique the writer leads the audience to understand the issues and appreciate how the data links directly to the conclusions and recommendations. This approach emphasises why something has happened and how it can be fixed. The essence of this style is cause and effect.

The problem solving approach sometimes relies on chronological reporting for elements that are far removed from the present situation. These elements are simply presented as background information. The current issues are described and presented in terms of their relative importance, with the cause and effect relationship highlighted. The recommendations follow directly in this same section where they are featured as the solution to the problems.

A long report should have a title page and a letter of transmittal. The title page includes the name of the person presenting the report and his/her affiliation, the name of the person who is receiving the report and his/her affiliation, the title of the report and the date of submission. The letter of transmittal identifies the report, the sender, the recipient, and suggestions regarding how the readers might obtain follow-up information. In addition, if the report is more than seven or eight pages and has more than four sections, a table of contents is appropriate.

3.10.3. Proposals

A proposal is a detailed offer of a product, service, or combination of these, usually for a few Good proposals are "sales" documents. They promise delivery of specified goods or services for compensation. Because proposals are designed to sell something, they must be drafted with a view towards presenting the best side of your organisation, your products and services, and your pricing. Clarity and brevity are particularly important. The reader will need to understand very explicitly just what you are promising. And, if the proposal is lengthier than expected, it won't be read.

Some proposals are written in response to an RFP (Request for proposal). RFP's are issued by organisations that want to solicit proposals that conform to set standards. The RFP will describe the way in which the proposal is to be organised, the information that is to be contained in the proposal, the way in which the proposal will be evaluated, deadlines for submission and evaluation, as well as financial, human resource and product constraints. In this way the RFP provides the blueprint for the proposal, describing how it is to be set out and what information it must contain.

When responding to an RFP, it is most important to provide the required information in the stated format, and to take all constraints into account. This requires careful reading of the RFP. Although this may sound self-evident, many submissions made in response to RFP's demonstrate that the proposal writer either did not read the RFP from cover to cover, or chose to ignore the information contained therein. Both of these are fatal errors. With many RFP's, the field of proposals is narrowed by as much as 50 per cent simply by rejecting those that do not reflect the requirements described in the RFP. The most important aspect of responding to an RFP is making sure you provide the information that has been requested in the format that is required.

Think of an RFP as an advertisement for a job. However, instead of presenting yourself in response to the advertisement, you are presenting your organisation, your products and services and the level of compensation you require. All of this is done in writing since few RFP processes involve face-to-face presentations. As is the case when applying for a job, you must work hard at detailing the skills and experience of your organisation. You would read a job advertisement very carefully, and try to find out more about the organisation that placed the advertisement and its needs. Similarly, you need to know as much as possible about the organisation tendering the RFP in order to write the winning proposal. Although RFP's vary in approach, most require several very specific elements.

- First, there is usually a requirement for a description of your organisation (or you, if the project is quite small), and the available human, financial and physical resources.

- Second, RFP's typically require a detailed section on the history of the organisation and its personnel, highlighting their success delivering similar projects. This is the "test of past success", a critical element in the mix since most projects are awarded to organisations that have demonstrated success. The underlying philosophy that drives this approach is the belief that the best predictor of future success is success in the past. Also taken in to account is the belief that it isn't the organisation that makes a project a success, it's the people in the organisation.

- Third, RFP's usually require a detailed description of the approach your organisation will use to deliver the project. In most cases this requires a detailed outline of the personnel and equipment that will be involved, as well as a timeline. If the project is service driven as opposed to being product focused, a great deal of attention will be placed on the people and their individual and cumulative experience.

Finally, a complete line-by-line costing of the project elements is usually required. This means detailing personnel costs, equipment allocations, and profit margins. The sponsoring organisation is particularly interested in determining how money is allocated since this provides another way in which the strength of your organisation can be evaluated. For this reason, it is not enough to simply indicate that you will meet the budget requirements; you must clarify how you will do this.

The proposal writer tries to make a case that external delivery could result in major benefits such as cost savings or increased product quality. For example, an educational institution might submit a proposal to supply retraining or upgrading for industry personnel, and the training department of the organisation might currently deliver that training. If the institution makes the case that it can deliver the training for less money or in a more effective manner, or both, the industry would almost certainly take a serious look at the proposal.

Unsolicited proposals should follow the format described earlier. Identify the problem or opportunity, describe the history and experience of your organisation, detail the approach that will be taken to deal with the issue, and summarise the financial aspects. All proposals, whether they are solicited or unsolicited, should be presented in a neat, clean, professional style.

Following are key points to remember when writing proposals:

- Read the RFP carefully.
- Provide all of the detail requested in the required format.
- Document your previous success.
- Back up all claims, preferably using concrete examples.
- Use a professional presentation style.

3.10.4 Traditional Mail

Postal systems date back to the Egyptians in 2000 B.C. The basic function has remained essentially the same, which is to allow parties separated by time and space to communicate with one another. Historically, the mail system was one of the fastest methods of communication, but with new technologies, it is now among the slowest. Moreover, with the rising costs of physical transport as opposed to electronic impulses and the labour expense of composing, typing and copying, the mail system is one of the more expensive communication channels. On the other hand, the very expense involved may convey to the receiver the importance of the message. A letter clearly is one of the most formal means of communication. Used in conjunction with word processing equipment, form letters can reach a large number of people who are geographically separated. These advantages of traditional mail often can outweigh difficulties with time lags and expenses.

3.10.5 Facsimile Machines

Facsimile or fax machines are rapidly replacing the traditional mail or "snail mail" it is sometimes called. Indeed, fax accounts for 50 per cent of all the telephone traffic between the United States and Japan. "The process is best described as putting a paper original in a fax machine", dialing the emotional and contextual components of messages more effectively than most written channels.

3.10.6 Electronic Mail

Electronic mail, or E-mail, is an asynchronous method of electronically transmitting text from one computer terminal to another. An employee can instantaneously send a message to another employees 'mailbox' and it will be read at the receiver's leisure. Most systems have a broadcast feature that allows the sender to 'zap' the message to any of a number of different distribution lists. Some systems even are designed so that the message sender can determine if the electronic message has been read or not. This is a capability that is not available with most written documents.

E-mail systems are probably best at communicating brief, noncomplex, but time sensitive information. It is hard to imagine much persuasion or negotiation going on through an E-mail system. In order to work, there needs to be critical mass of users who are separated geographically but have easy access to their own computers. Even sharing a terminal with one other user has been shown to decrease commitment to E-mail. Some networks provide slick devices to get around a few of difficulties but, in the final analysis, the effectiveness of this channel comes down to the skills and commitment of the people using it.

3.11 Group Communication

College students in today's highly organised urban society often find themselves communicating in small groups for several hours each day. We live in a time when group techniques are widely used to teach many different subjects. Instructors often group students to work on assignments. More and more, teachers are encouraged to break classes into smaller groups to study for examinations or to prepare for classes.

Much of our recreational and social life is related to groups. How often in a day or a week do groups carry on casual social conversations? How often do people go in groups to a party, a concert, or a movie? Group's relationships increase understanding of social give and take and make people more sensitive to one another. Some groups are designed to help individuals deal with job related stress or personal problems. The strength and support groups set up to help people deal with daily stresses and problems are often similar to the therapy groups that help alcoholics, drugs addicts, juvenile delinquents, and the mentally ill.

The study of small group communication is important not only to familiarise with the way people communicate together to share information, set goals, make plans, solve problems, make decisions, and grow in understanding, but also with the way they create social bonds, status and power relationships, cliques and factions, animosities and hostilities.

Group communication involves three or more persons. The smaller the number in the group, the more closely this mode resembles interpersonal communication. Often group communication is done for the purpose of problem solving or decision-making. Example: University study group.

Much communication takes place in the context of small groups, which are defined as those of three or more participants. The various and overlapping types of small groups lead to various types of communication patterns.

- Social groups are units such as families, friends living as roommates, and voluntary recreational groups such as soccer teams.

- Families also form primary groups, which are defined as those in which people share living and financial arrangements.

- Families also are an example of reference groups, through which participants gain a sense of identity and an awareness of expected behaviour.

- Work groups are another pattern of relationships. These are built by people who are drawn together by a common task, such as students working together on a project or company employees assigned to a common job activity.

- Decision-making groups are brought together for the purpose of dealing with a question or policy.

- Similarly though distinctly, problem-solving groups focus on resolving a problem. The working of groups has been the subject of much study, particularly from the framework of organisational communication. Leadership styles of small groups have been identified - generally in a three-part continuum ranging from high control (authoritarian leaders) through moderate control (democratic leaders) to low control (laissez-faire leaders). A fourth type, called abdicate, involves the total collapse of leadership over uncontrolled group dynamics. Psychologists and communication scholars have observed a pattern of group development, usually presented in a four-fold model.

- The process begins with an orientation phase in which participants get to know each other and learn what is expected of them as a group.

- In the conflict phase, they deal with sources of conflict, usually in an effort to avoid conflict within the group. Too much conflict can prevent the group from functioning. However, some conflict is useful to avoid the pressure toward conformity known as groupthink.

- This norm emergence phase centres on compromise, the convergence of ideas, generation of alternative solutions, and eventually consensus. A technique often used to enhance the early part of this phase is brainstorming, in which unrestrained possible solutions and options are generated with no self-censorship or initial group evaluation. The purpose of brainstorming is to generate as many ideas as possible. Only after the ideas have been generated will they be evaluated, keeping the two steps separate and thus allowing the group to consider all possible options.

- The closure phase completes the process by concluding the group's work.

3.12 Kinds of Discussions

Group discussions are held for a variety of reasons and may take several different forms. A group discussion may deal with education, social welfare, civil rights, urban problems, consumerism, politics, war and peace, the arts, or any number of public and intellectual issues. Educators and broadcasters, among the most frequent participants of public discussions often use fresh approaches to the organisation of programme and meetings. Organisers of public discussions and conferences and workshops constantly search for the gimmick or some novel twist to add interest to their discussions.

Public discussions generally differ from programme such as lectures and presentations in their informality and in the number of participants. The informality of the public discussion format tends to break down social tensions and allows listeners to enjoy the interplay of ideas and personalities. The various kinds of discussions are categorised as under.

3.12.1 Public Discussions

Public discussions are group meetings that present material to an audience. Such discussions may take place before a live audience, on radio, or before television cameras. Public discussions generally are more carefully planned than are private discussions. Participants plan the details of organisation of material; turn taking, and time limits.

3.12.2 Forum Discussions

Public-discussion programme may allow for audience questions and comments, in which case they are called forum discussions. Public discussions have a chairperson or moderator who introduces both the topic and participants to the audience and moderates the audience participating during the forum section.

3.12.3 Conference Discussions

Conference discussions are group meetings that are used as part of a learning conference or workshop. A large group of participants may come together for intensive study of some theme or some common problem. The group may listen to lectures, view audio-visual presentations, or participate in role-playing exercises. The participants often will alternate such conference techniques with small group discussions in which they process their experiences, share their knowledge, and further clarify their understandings of the conference proceedings.

3.12.4 Symposium Discussions

The opening part of the discussion programme may be organised as a symposium discussion. In a symposium discussion members divide the topic among themselves. Each member makes a brief comment about his or her subdivision of the topic after the moderator introduces the programme. Opening speeches are usually carefully prepared, timed and uninterrupted. Following the round of opening comments, the discussion may become a forum with everyone participating, or the discussants may take a few minutes to question one another about the content of their speeches.

3.12.5 Panel Discussions

The opening part of the discussion programme may be organised as a Panel Discussion. In the panel discussion, all participants take part in discussing each point on the programme outline. The atmosphere of the panel is less formal than that of the symposium and members interrupt one another as they aim to create the illusion spontaneity and give and take of a typical work meeting. The main difference between the panel discussion and a work group meeting is that the programme is carefully planned as to agenda and amount of time to be devoted to each portion of the programme.

A good procedure is to devote about half of the time to the panel discussion and then follow with a forum period.

A radio or television discussion is often in the form of a panel, sometimes with the studio audience and sometimes without. The participants typically sit around the studio and speak informally with one another. Radio and television discussion are excellent ways to deal with important questions. The informality and spontaneity of the format make for good listener interest. Over the years, particularly on television, informal discussion formats have grown in popularity when compared to prepared, formal public speeches.

3.12.6 Private Discussions

Private discussions consist of group of people who come together to discuss a topic without inviting an audience. They may wish to explore a problem, study an issue or discuss ideas in a learning context for the benefit of the group members. Instructors may form student groups to discuss a novel, a film or a set of assigned readings. A small group of interested citizens may meet to discuss community problems.

3.12.7 Group Discussion

Group discussion is an early perspective on small group communication; it began some sixty years ago in departments of speech communication. In the beginning the group discussion courses were oriented towards discussion as a tool for social control. Specifically, the public discussion of important public issues was a way to educate people for their roles as citizens in a democracy. Discussion informed audience (as citizens in a democracy) of basic problems and enabled them to hear all sides of a controversy. Discussion is a good way to mold public opinion and make decisions. Public discussion as a means of social control can be contrasted with other methods such as verdict, orders backed by the threat of force, or the manipulation of public opinion by mass influence.

Freedom of speech is a basic assumption required for the successful use of public discussion as a method of decision-making in a democracy. Opinions should be allowed a fair hearing. If all points of view are presented the people will distinguish truth from error. The suppression of unpopular ideas may be unwise because they may contain truth; if the public is searching for truth, the majority must not by prior censorship shut off any possible avenue to knowledge. However, even if the unpopular ideas are false, they should not be censored because the old familiar truths lose their vitality unless they are periodically challenged and defended. When old ideas are challenged, even if they service the challenge, the process revitalises them.

Another assumption of the group discussion approach is that people can vote and act wisely if given an opportunity. By means of public discussion they are given a chance to hear all sides of important public questions. Another assumption that grows naturally from the concept of the wisdom of the public is that the individual is important in his or her own right and not a component in the machine of the state or a means toward an ulterior end. Therefore, people have a right to participate in their own destiny. They should not be manipulated and treated as though their humaneness is unimportant. They should be consulted about decisions that affect their welfare. Finally the use of public discussion as a technique of social control also assumes that people, although they frequently commit irrational acts, are capable of acting rationally and basing some of their decisions on good reason. Further it assumes that such rational decisions are the best decisions that people make. The conclusion then follows that training in public discussion, with heavy emphasis on discovering the facts and drawing sound inferences from them, is also training for democratic citizenship.

The early courses in public discussion used the concepts of the scientist and the scientific attitude as the model for the participant in public discussion. Participants, according to this perspective, were to adopt the scientific attitude, to be open-minded to welcome differences of opinion, to accept challenges to their own thinking and to remain objective and uninvolved when evaluating ideas and facts. The proper attitude to bring in to the discussion was one that adapted a scientific approach to the discussion of social and political problems - such an attitude was called the discussion attitude.

The human relations dimension of group discussion is essentially encompassed in the concept of the discussion attitude. The discussion attitude is a reflection of the emphasis on the systematic approach to the reasonable process of inquiry and to thinking. The discussant with the discussion attitude is open-minded and in contrast to the debater, persuader, or propagandist, is willing to go where the facts lead. A participant outfit has a tentative position on the question under discussion but would not have an emotional investment in his or her own ideas. In addition, good discussant has an attitude of not allowing emotional responses to affect their reasoning or their ability to think reflectively.

A group discussion contemplates having one of the participants exercise the role of moderator or discussion guide. This role may include most of the details of planning and organising the programme, then conducting the actual meeting introducing participants, handling audience questions or comments, and controlling the turn taking. The moderator acts as a lot to keep the group on the agenda, to handle special problems such as the too talkative or too silent member, and to achieve a good discussion.

The role of participant in a group discussion is to be well prepared on the topic in question, to participate fully, and to integrate the participation into the overall flow of the discussion. All participants are expected to be properly objective and cooperative in their discussion and to express their ideas in clear language with good use of voice, expression and gesture.

The human relations aspect of group process was given relatively little attention in theorizing about group discussion. It also became apparent that it was very difficult given the dynamics of group process, for individual to follow the steps of the discussion process while actually hard at work on a problem. With growing interest in task oriented group work in committees, task forces, and organisational work groups, courses in discussion began to de-emphasise public discussions and to emphasise the more private continuing task oriented group with common problems to solve and decisions to make.

Gradually, the accumulation of research on to the dynamics and processes of small task oriented groups resulted in the development of a perspective on small group communication. This perspective integrated research findings with an approach to teaching about and participating in groups that emphasised the socio-emotional and task dimension.

Despite shifting emphasis on the types and nature of task-oriented small groups, the material dealing with group discussion has a continuing role to play in the study of groups and communication.

3.13 Kinds of Meetings

3.13.1 The one Time Meeting

People who expect to achieve their purpose in a single meeting hold the one-time meeting. People in the one time meeting typically have not worked together before and are not likely to do so again for the purposes under discussion. The meeting may take place in an organisational context, but is often used for community purposes. Representatives from several different organisations or interest groups may come to one-time meetings to discuss a common problem, share information, or plan a joint enterprise.

Since the composition of the one-time meetings is unique, the group has no history and members cannot be guided by past experience with one another. The group has no team spirit, no "usual" ways of doing things, no idea about how the communication and social interactions will go. One of the important things about the one-time meeting is the usual willingness of members to accept assigned leadership. Whether the person calling the meeting is a self appointed moderator or has been assigned to lead by some organisational unit, the members are likely to accept and appreciate direction from that individual. The group conducting a one-time meeting needs quick help in getting started. Members realise that they have little time to get on with the meeting and tend to accept with little arguments the assigned moderator description of the purposes of the meeting and his or her set of procedures.

Members in a one-time meeting take shortcuts to structure their group into a packing order so that they can get on with the business at hand. They are willing to risk getting a wrong impression because they are pressed for time and because the group is to short-lived to invest the time and energy it takes to test out rules and procedures.

Once a one time discussion gets under way, participants use any information they have about one another to structure their responses. If, for instance, participants discover that one member is a student of nursing, another a student in speech communication, and a third a law student, they use such information to guide their expectations. Participants who are not known by reputation are quickly stereotyped on the basis of first impressions and whatever limited information others have. A person who does not say much for the first ten or fifteen minutes may be stereotyped as quiet and shy or uninterested. Another, who speaks loudly, expresses strong opinions and makes flat judgments, may be stereotyped as bossy or pushy.

3.13.2 The Ad-Hoc Committee Meeting

The ad-hoc committee is different from the one time discussion meeting. Ad hoc is a Latin term meaning "for this special purpose." An ad-hoc committee is set up for a given task and usually meets for several sessions. For very important tasks the ad-hoc committee may meet over a period of weeks or months.

The ad-hoc committee is like the one time meeting in that both are zero-history groups, but the ad-hoc committee has a future. Members look forward to having more meetings and the influence of expectations often makes them caution about supporting ideas, plans and people. The zero history groups with a future is under pressure to test potential leaders and other possibly influential members, to develop norms, to take nothing at face value, to check reputations, formal organisation status, and assigned structures before accepting them. The small groups communication perspective is more appropriate for the ad-hoc committee than is the group-discussion approach.

The person who agrees to serve on an ad-hoc committee must understand the important expectation we are stressing. People become involved when they must work on ad-hoc committees, whether they plan to or not.

3.13.3 Negotiating Groups

Our stress here is upon the task-oriented small group that puts emphasis upon cooperation among members to achieve a common goal and to share in the value achieved from their common success. Some groups, however, are clearly in communication situations that emphasis competition. When representatives from two groups or organisations in conflict meet to work out an agreement, despite the fact that they have conflicting goals, the result is a negotiating session.

The communication climate of a negotiating meeting puts a premium on misleading, confusing, and bluffing the other side. Neither message nor relationship communication is appropriate to the negotiating session. Where relationship communication emphasises the honest nonverbal expression of internal feelings. The negotiating session emphasises the nonverbal masking of internal feelings. The poker face and tantrum are useful nonverbal techniques when negotiators are testing one another with offers and counter offers.

, The high-fidelity communication of the message model is in appropriate to negotiations where participants want to discover as much as they can about what the other side is willing to agree to and how strongly the other side wants an agreement. Negotiator try to read between the lines, interpret inadvertent nonverbal giveaways, make other assessments of the "last offer" of the other side, and at the same time keep the opponents in the dark about their own objectives. Good faith bargaining is often the ideal but can easily degenerate into bad faith. In any case, the communication context is competitive and resembles legal litigation much more than small group communication.

Our purpose here is not to set out a theory of negotiating communication but simply to note that groups sometimes meet around a table in a session that might on the surface seem to be a task oriented cooperative group when, in fact, the people are bargaining and negotiating.

3.13.4 Planning the Meeting

Be sure a meeting is needed: Some meetings are held for no good reason. Perhaps originally a periodic meeting may have served a function but, as time goes by, the organisation has changed and the meeting has lost its purpose; yet it is still held out of habit. Meetings are also used as administrative dodges; an administrator can evade a touchy issue by burying it in committee. An authoritarian administrator may use a meeting as a smoke screen for a decision already made by pretending that the meeting will make it. After a time, the people in the meeting catch on to what is happening. They know that the meeting is simply a show that the "old man" has already made up his mind and that nothing said in the meeting will change things. Such meetings are a waste of time.

Do not have a meeting unless it is absolutely necessary. Meetings are the heavy artillery of an organisation's communications. A wise general uses his heavy artillery sparingly because it is expensive and difficult to maneuver. On the other hand, when he does need his big guns, he really has no satisfactory substitute for them. If individual conferences, telephone conversations, memorandums, or other techniques can handle communication, the meeting is probably unnecessary.

Determine the Purpose of the Meeting: Every meeting should have a clear and specific purpose. Those who attend it should know the purpose either before the meeting starts or very early in the session.

Plan the Meeting to Achieve the Purpose: Where is the best place to hold the meeting? What format will best achieve the purpose? Is a slide lecture with questions and answers best for a briefing session? Would short reports, followed by questions and answers, be appropriate for a consultative meeting? Could a round-table discussion of an agenda be used for policy making? Who should take part in the meeting? Should people with special knowledge be invited? Should some high-status people be invited to keep fences ready within the organisation? Might the outcome be jeopardising if some one felt hurt because he was not informed or consulted? Who should chair the meeting?

Plan the Little Details: A successful meeting requires time and effort in the planning stages. To neglect the planning may save time for someone in a hurry, but wasting the time of his colleagues in a useless meeting is not wise. Little things like providing pads and pencils, refreshments, properly arranged (and sufficient) seating - all these contribute to the success of the meeting. When minor details of administration are handled smoothly, the people get the feeling that the meeting is important and that they are going to do significant work.

Specify the Outcomes of the Meeting: Outcomes are not the same as purposes. If plans are to be made, how will they be developed? In detail? In general outline? What decisions can be made in the meeting and what form should they be made?

Utilise the Results of the Meeting: The substantive results of the meeting should be used. What can be done to follow up and apply the results of the conference? Important leads should never be allowed to drop at the end of the meeting.

Evaluate the Meeting Systematically: Some time should be invested in evaluating the effectiveness of the meeting. People often make an informal evaluation of a meeting as they walk away from it. They may say to someone else, or to themselves, that it was a good meeting, that the members talked all around the subject, or that it was a waste of time. What we have in mind is a more careful and systematic evaluation. Some member of the group should collect impressions of the strengths and weaknesses of the meeting. These evaluations should be fed back to the participants.

One of the striking discoveries in the study of groups is that they seldom spend any time talking about the group and about how it functions. Groups tend to concentrate on the job and ignore the important matters discussed. When groups do spend short periods after the meeting talking as a group, about what happened in the meeting, about what was good and what was bad, the cohesiveness and effectiveness of the meeting are increased. Often things that are very disturbing when hidden from others evaporate when brought out onto the open and discussed. Perhaps one person with some education in group process should be asked to serve as an evaluator of the meeting, and that person can present a systematic statement to start the discussion.

3.13.5. Teleconferencing

The teleconference is the telephone equivalent of the group meeting. Small or large groups can simultaneously communicate in a single conversation via the phone line. The channel provides, in some cases, an economical alternative to travel for managers who need to participate in a discussion with people who are geographically separated. Sometimes preliminary selection interviews are conducted with applicants via teleconference.

Despite the widespread availability of teleconferencing, it has not replaced travel because of some obvious limitations, such as the lack of a visual component. A more subtle limitation is that secondary conversations are discouraged in this medium. During face-to-face group meetings involving more than four or five people, there are usually other conversations occurring simultaneously in smaller groups of two or three. Since a single phone line transmits the communication in a teleconference. Secondary conversations often are avoided, which may mean some valuable information is not shared or, if they do occur, time is taken away from the primary discussion. Participants may get background on some topic that is of little concern to them. Either way the net effect can be detrimental. On the other hand, the elimination of some secondary conversations may actually speed up the process and make participants focus more on the task than is possible in a traditional meeting. In short, a teleconference offers an efficient alternative to many face-to-face group conferences, but it does not totally simulate one.

3.14 Non-verbal Communication

By non-verbal communication, we mean all communication that involves neither written nor spoken words but occurs without the use of words. Our definition is broad enough to include non-verbal communication that occurs together with verbal communication as well as non-verbal communication that occurs alone. In contrast, verbal communication involves words. In non-verbal (non word) communication, we are concerned with such things as body movements, space, time and voice rhythm/ inflection as well as general characteristics of the environment, colour and layout/design.

Non-verbal communication is usually understood as the process of communication through sending and receiving wordless (mostly visual) messages. Messages can be communicated through gestures, by body language or posture, by facial expression and eye contact. Meaning can also be communicated through object or artifacts (such as clothing, hairstyles or architecture). Speech contains non-verbal elements known as paralanguage, including voice quality, rate, pitch, volume, and speaking style, as well as prosodic features such as rhythm, tone and stress. Likewise, written texts have non-verbal elements such as handwriting style, spatial arrangement of words, or the physical layout of a page. Dance is also regarded as a form of non-verbal communication.

However, much of the study of non-verbal communication has focused on face-to-face interaction, where it can be classified into three principal areas: environmental conditions where communication takes place, physical characteristics of the communicators, and behaviours of communicators during interaction.

What is Non-verbal Communication?

Definition "non-verbal communication involves those non-verbal stimuli in a communication setting that are generated by both the source [speaker] and his or her use of the environment and that have potential message value for the source or receiver [listener]". Basically it is sending and receiving messages in a variety of ways without the use of verbal codes (words). It is both intentional and unintentional. Most speakers/listeners are not conscious of this. It includes -- but is not limited to:

- touch
- glance
- eye contact (gaze)
- volume
- vocal nuance
- proximity
- gestures
- facial expression ? pause (silence)
- intonation
- dress
- posture
- smell
- word choice and syntax
- sounds (paralanguage)

Broadly speaking, there are two basic categories of non-verbal language: (i) nonverbal messages produced by the body; (ii) nonverbal messages produced by the broad setting (time, space, and silence).

Why is Non-verbal Communication Important?

Basically, it is one of the key aspects of communication (and especially important in a high-context culture). It has multiple functions:

- Used to repeat the verbal message (e.g., point in a direction while stating directions.
- Often used to accent a verbal message. (e.g., verbal tone indicates the actual meaning of the specific wonrds).
- Often complement the verbal message but also may contradict. E.g., a nod reinforces a positive message (among Americans); a "wink" may contradict a stated positive message.
- Regulate interactions (non-verbal cues convey when the other person should speak or not speak).
- May substitute for the verbal message (especially if it is blocked by noise, interruption, etc), i.e., gestures (finger to lips to indicate need for quiet), facial expressions (i.e., a nod instead of a yes).

Note the implications of the proverb: "Actions speak louder than words." In essence, this underscores the importance of non-verbal communication. Non-verbal communication is especially significant in intercultural situations. Probably non-verbal differences account for typical difficulties in communicating.

Cultural Differences in Non-verbal Communication

1. **General Appearance and Dress** – All cultures are concerned for how they look and make judgments based on looks and dress. Americans, for instance, appear almost obsessed with dress and personal attractiveness. Consider differing cultural

standards on what is attractive in dress and on what constitutes modesty. Note ways dress is used as a sign of status?

2. **Body Movement** - We send information on attitude toward person (facing or leaning towards another), emotional statue (tapping fingers, jiggling coins), and desire to control the environment (moving towards or away from a person). More than 700,000 possible motions we can make, so impossible to categorise them all! But just need to be aware the body movement and position is a key ingredient in sending messages.

3. **Posture** - Consider the following actions and note cultural differences:

   - Bowing (not done, criticised, or affected in US; shows rank in Japan)
   - Slouching (rude in most Northern European areas)
   - Hands in pocket (disrespectful in Turkey)
   - Sitting with legs crossed (offensive in Ghana, Turkey)
   - Showing soles of feet. (Offensive in Thailand, Saudi Arabia)
   - Even in US, there is a gender difference on acceptable posture?

4. **Gestures** - Impossible to catalog them all. But need to recognise: (1) incredible possibility and variety and (2) that an acceptable in one's own culture may be offensive in another. In addition, amount of gesturing varies from culture to culture. Some cultures are animated; other restrained. Restrained cultures often feel animated cultures lack manners and overall restraint. Animated cultures often feel restrained cultures lack emotion or interest. Even simple things like using hands to point and count differ for e.g. (i) Pointing: US with index finger; Germany with little finger;

Japanese with entire hand (in fact most Asians consider pointing with index finger to be rude). (ii) Counting: Thumb = 1 in Germany, 5 in Japan, middle finger for 1 in Indonesia.

5. **Facial Expressions** - While some say that facial expressions are identical, meaning attached to them differs. Majority opinion is that these do have similar meanings worldwide with respect to smiling, crying, or showing anger, sorrow, or disgust. However, the intensity varies from culture to culture. Note the following:

- Many Asian cultures suppress facial expression as much as possible.
- Many Mediterranean (Latino / Arabic) cultures exaggerate grief or sadness while most American men hide grief or sorrow.
- Some see "animated" expressions as a sign of a lack of control.
- Too much smiling is viewed in as a sign of shallowness.
- Women smile more than men.

6. **Eye Contact and Gaze** - In USA, eye contact indicates: degree of attention or interest, influences attitude change or persuasion, regulates interaction, communicates emotion, defines power and status, and has a central role in managing impressions of others.

- Western cultures — see direct eye to eye contact as positive (advise children to look a person in the eyes). But within USA, African-Americans use more eye contact when talking and less when listening with reverse true for Anglo Americans. This is a possible cause for some sense of unease between races in US. A prolonged gaze is often seen as a sign of sexual interest.
- Arabic cultures make prolonged eye contact. — believe it shows interest and helps them understand truthfulness

of the other person. (A person who doesn't reciprocate is seen as untrustworthy)

- Japan, Africa, Latin American, Caribbean — avoid eye contact to show respect.

7. **Touch** - Question: Why do we touch, where do we touch, and what meanings do we assign when someone else touches us? Illustration: An African-American male goes into a convenience store recently taken over by new Korean immigrants. He gives a $20 bill for his purchase to Mrs Cho who is cashier and waits for his change. He is upset when his change is put down on the counter in front of him.

   What is the problem? Traditional Korean (and many other Asian countries) don't touch strangers, especially between members of the opposite sex. But the African-American sees this as another example of discrimination (not touching him because he is black).

   Basic answer: Touch is culturally determined! But each culture has a clear concept of what parts of the body one may not touch. Basic message of touch is to affect or control — protect, support, disapprove (i.e. hug, kiss, hit, kick).

   - USA — handshake is common (even for strangers), hugs, kisses for those of opposite gender or of family (usually) on an increasingly more intimate basis. Note differences between African-Americans and Anglos in USA. Most African Americans touch on greeting but are annoyed if touched on the head (good boy, good girl overtones).

   - Islamic and Hindu: typically don't touch with the left hand. To do so is a social insult. Left hand is for toilet functions. Mannerly in India to break your bread only with your right hand (sometimes difficult for non-Indians).

   - Islamic cultures generally don't approve of any touching between genders (even hand shakes). But consider such touching (including hand holding, hugs) between same-sex to be appropriate.

- Many Asians don't touch the head (Head houses the soul and a touch puts it in jeopardy).

Basic patterns: Cultures (English, German, Scandinavian, Chinese, Japanese) with high emotional restraint concepts have little public touch; those encourage emotion (Latino, Middle-East, Jewish) accept frequent touches.

8. Smell

- USA — fear of offensive natural smells (billion dollar industry to mask objectionable odours with what is perceived to be pleasant) — again connected with "attractiveness" concept.

- Many other cultures consider natural body odours as normal (Arabic).

- Asian cultures (Filipino, Malay, Indonesian, Thai, Indian) stress frequent bathing — and often criticise USA of not bathing often enough!

9. Paralanguage

- Vocal characterises (laugh, cry, yell, moan, whine, belch, yawn). These send different messages in different cultures (Japan — giggling indicates embarrassment; India - belch indicates satisfaction).

- Vocal qualifiers (volume, pitch, rhythm, tempo, and tone). Loudness indicates strength in Arabic cultures and softness indicates weakness; indicates confidence and authority to the Germans; indicates impoliteness to the Thais; indicates loss of control to the Japanese. (Generally, one learns not to "shout" in Asia for nearly any reason!). Gender based as well: women tend to speak higher and more softly than men.

- Vocal segregates (un-huh, shh, uh, ooh, mmmh, humm, eh, mah, lah). Segregates indicate formality, acceptance, assent, and uncertainty.

3.14.1 Classification of Non-verbal Communication Modes

As we have seen, the field of non-verbal communication is quite inclusive. To make its study meaningful to us, therefore, we must break it down by category. Thus, we will explore the various subparts of non-verbal communication: (A) Kinesics (B) Proxemics (C) The language (D) Paralanguage, and (E) Physical context.

(A) Kinesics

We can define kinesics as the study of the body's physical movements. In other words, it is the way the body communicates without words that are through various movements of its parts. When we study kinesics. We specifically look for inner states of emotion as expressed through different parts of the body and their physical movements. By nodding your head, blinking your eyes, shrugging your shoulders, waving your hands, and making other such physical movements, you send messages to others.

When we study body "language", we are looking at symbols of meaning that the body's physical movements are communicating We are searching for attitudes, perceived status relationships, moods, deception, warmth, needs for interaction and the like as body symbols and activities express them. Of course, we must infer these meanings from symbols because we do not see exactly what they stand for. But outward body movements reflect true inner conditions of meaning. We look for expressions of these inner body states in the:

- Face and eyes
- Gestures
- Posture, and
- Physical appearance

Face and Eyes

By air, the face is where we look for most expressions of what is going on inside us. Within the facial area, the eyes tell us much more than other facial features. Thus, we look to the face and eyes when we want to determine much of the meaning behind body language and non-verbal communication. For example, consider the facial expressions you associate with happiness, surprise, fear, anger and sadness. Do you look to the mouth, jaw, eyes, nose, cheeks, or forehead for your decision? Is the mouth open wide or closed, the eyelid raised or lowered, the nose wrinkled or relaxed, the cheeks drawn up back, the forehead lowered or raised? All of the facial parts combined tell you something about what is happening to create the expressions you see. For evidence of these ideas, you might look at a magazine advertisement containing people to determine the extent to which each part of their faces fits together to "depict" various emotional states.

Better still, look in a mirror and see how your own face reflects what is going on within you at the moment. Express to yourself different emotions and see how your jaws, mouth, nose, eyes, cheeks and forehead respond to each. If you can record your expressions on videotape, you can study them in even more detail. The automatic ways in which the facial parts react may surprise you.

As we noted, the facial feature to which we look most for meaning is the eyes. The eyes, along with the eyebrows. Upper and lower eyelids, and size of pupils, convey certain inner body states. Eyebrows with upper and lower eyelids raised combined with deleted pupils—a wide-eyed effect—tells us that the person is excited, surprised, or frightened. The opposite effect eyebrows with upper and lower eyelids closed (less white space exposed combine with contracted pupils—a beady-eyed look tell us that the person is angry, intense or in pain. When these eye features are put together with other facial parts, we infer about the persons inner going on.

While eye patterns communicate to us, eye contact (gazing) and movements are also meaningful. If we look at someone or something for a long period of time, we show our intensity of interest. Brief eye contact generally reveals embarrassment, timidity, or nervousness. Of course, eye contact and movement must be placed within the context of other facial expressions and body movements to get a total meaning. Yet eye contact and eye movements indeed help significantly in the filtering process.

Gestures

In addition to the face and eyes, other body parts move and convey meaning. We refer to these movements as gestures - the physical movements of arms, legs, hands, upper body and head. Because we have just examined the face and eyes, we will exclude the head for the moment and concentrate on other body movements.

For example of gestures, consider first some common hand and finger movements—a pounding fist on a table, a forefinger held above an athlete's head, a forefinger and a thumb touching to form a circle. Indeed, you probably associate "anger". "Number 1" and "OK" with these gestures, respectively. Likewise, arms spread far apart, shuffling from one leap to the other, and a body torso erect and extended slightly forward convey meanings of "wide", "nervous" and "intense". To be sure, we can conclude that gestures tell us something about people's internal emotional states. But we must modify this conclusion with some additional ideas about gestures and their meanings.

Researchers who study gestures generally believe that gestures are made relationally: That is, they are used not individually but in relation to another person. Thus, certain gesture have meaning at particular times in an interpersonal situation - at the beginning, middle, and end of the interchange. To get the true meaning of the gestures used in an interpersonal relationship, we must look at the specific situation of the relationship.

Also speaking and gesturing appear to be linked, although the nature of the linkage is not exactly known. Generally intensity of speech appears to be directly associated with the size of a gesture: the greater the gesture, the lauder the speech vice versa. We appear to continually attempt to coordinate our speaking with our gestures. Because speech and gestures are both learned, we also learn how to coordinate them. When the two are uncoordinated, we experience discomfort and confusion.

Body Shape and Posture

A third area of kinesics involves body shape and posture. Because body shape and posture affect how we think about ourselves, how we relate to others, and how others relate to us, this part of kinesics deserves our analysis. We need to analyze the effects of body shape and posture to understand their role in non-verbal communication, even though body shape is mostly hereditary and largely uncontrollable.

Consider, for example, the last meeting you had with a close friend. What was it like when you first met? If you are like most people, you were probably spontaneous. You likely were unaware of your posture during the meeting, being fluid in all of your physical movements. But in contrast, with a situation less familiar to you—say an interview for an important job or a formal speech. Here you are more aware of your posture, trying to make the best impression possible. Perhaps you feel awkward trying to maintain a formal standing or sitting position.

Holding your head straight, maintaining your upper body erect, standing on both feet, and sitting intently listening, you are more aware of your posture in the more formal setting. But posture is a part of any relationship, regardless of your degree of awareness. Whether you lean forward or backward, stand or sit erectly, or droop haphazardly, you tell another person something: and the others mental filter gives meaning to your posture.

Also, the physical shapes of our bodies communicate to others. Behaviourists have studied the shapes of our bodies and have identified three types. The ectomorph is thin, youthful, and tall; the mesomorph is strong, athletic, muscular, and bony; and the endomorph is fat, round, and soft. Indeed, our physical structures communicate something about us and we would do well to be aware of it. Perhaps these body types lead to false stereotypes, but the point remains that our physical structures do communicate.

Probably all of us would like to be mesomorphs, but that might be genetically or physically impossible. What do we do? We need to use the best features of each body shape in relation to other body movements. The endomorph with bad posture, superficial gestures and an unfriendly face will project, an unfavourable image. Such a person will likely communicate a negative message. So too can we associate negative features with the ectomorph and the mesomorph. Thus, we want to avoid such negative combinations and associations.

Appearance

The final area of kinesics is appearance. By appearance, we mean clothing, hair, and adornments such as jewellery, cosmetics and like. At first glance, it may seem that appearance is unrelated to body movements. Closer inspection, however, reveals that appearance relates to how the face, eyes, gestures, postures and shapes — all those aspects of body language we have discussed are perceived. Thus, we will present some basic ideas about appearance, although our coverage will not include etiquette or good grooming techniques.

If you are like most people, you are not aware of the role appearance plays in your perceptions. Most people indicate they are not influenced by another's physical appearance, but apparently they are. Our own and other's appearances tell us much about how we (and they) want to be seen by other people. They also reveal how we practice the "rules of the game" in an organisation.

As an example, consider how your fellow workers might respond to you if you suddenly changed your work dress from formal to informal - say, from professionally tailored clothing to blue jeans. To be sure, the change would tell something about you. All of a sudden, you would be different and you would stand out from others. This dramatic change would also convey your definition of the organisations work rules and whether you intended to abide by them or break them.

While this example is extreme, it illustrates the effect, of appearance on perception. More delicate forms would be wearing a sport coat versus a suit, changing heel size from high to low and the like. As still another illustration consider those times when you give your appearance special attention. When are they? How long does it take you to get ready for your day? What do you do? Answer to these types of questions will tell you much about the importance of appearance.

By now you surely see that appearance affects the way we are seen and want to be seen by others. Indeed, books on successful dressing and "image" consultants attest to the importance of appearance. Although there are many aspects to appearance the basic idea is this: You should adapt your appearance specifically to the one occasion.

You should consider how others would view you in relation to how you want to be seen. Just like other body features (face, eyes, hands, legs, arms, posture and shape), appearance is an inevitable part of the meaning derived from our body movements. You should expect appearance to be a part of the messages you communicate, and you should plan your appearance so that it will effectively communicate to others.

(B) Proxemics

Another type of non-verbal communication is proxemics - the study of how we communicate with the space around us. If you think about it carefully, you will conclude that the space around you and its contents communicate. They create meaning in your mind and in others minds. We can define proxemics, then, as the study of the space around us - how we arrange it and what we arrange in it. In other words, proxemics is "Personal space language" just as kinesics is "body language". To understand this concept, we will first look at an example; then we will examine the example based on what scholars of this subject have found. To illustrate the idea of space meaning, consider the area that surrounds you at this moment - the space from your body outward that forms a complete circle around you for about 1-½ feet. Remember that in this space you originate all of the body movements we discussed previously. Also, note that you move this space with you wherever you go. Whom do you allow to enter into this close proximity to you? Family? Close friends? Select others? Under what circumstance do others come into such closeness with you? More than likely, you permit only special people to enter this space; in general, no words or at most whispered words are used here. Others may enter this space occasionally but only under special circumstances. A handshake or a quick pat on the back are what you probably allow casual acquaintances to do in this space. But they enter this space infrequently and briefly.

Next, consider the space that extends from 1, 1/2 to 4 feet beyond the first space zone just identified. In this second, concentric space circle, you permit other and different things to happen. Conversations with close friends, colleagues, peers, and the like occur. Normal talking is permitted in this area as opposed to whispered words or complete silence in the more intimate space immediately surrounding you. Although personal in nature, it is a relaxed and casual place for you most of the time and permits spontaneous, un-programmed communications.

Extending beyond the second area is a third identifiable space zone. It begins at the 4-feet mark and continues for 8 more feet. Think about this personal space and what happens in it for a moment. More than likely, you use this space formally, meaning that the relationships in it are more official. No doubt most of your "business" is done in this zone, it is conducted with less emotion and more planning.

The last area to consider ranges from 12 feet around you to the farthest distance you can see. Things that occur here are even more formal. Perhaps you might view happenings in this area as an impartial observer. Such a perception indicates the degree of detachment you can maintain about activities in this area. You might have to raise your voice to communicate to others. This last area represents the most remote, the formal space for you. In some cases, it might be where you place the things that are least significant to you.

These four spaces are what Hall refers to as our informal space. Specifically, Hall names four types of informal space :

1. Intimate - physical contact to 18 inches.

2. Personal - 18 inches to 4 feet.

3. Social - 4 to 12 feet.

4. Public - 12 feet to range of eyesight and hearing.

Without question, the types and quality of our communication activities differ in each of these four zones, as we have illustrated. But remember that we determine these areas individually, and can change them by changing our physical location. Thus, they are specific to us personally. For another person these personal areas might be changed even more particularly if he or she has been conditioned by another culture. For instance, activities in the first zone may differ dramatically between a person in North America and another in the Middle East. More suitable differences may exist, however, among people raised in the same culture.

In addition to informal space researchers, have identified two other spaces: (1) fixed space and (2) semi-fixed space. As their names imply, they are less flexible and more formal for us than our informal spaces. But the two fixed spaces do relate to our uses of space language as we have defined it, and they help shape our communication activities.

In fixed space, the surroundings physical features are permanent - walls, room sizes, total building capacity, and the like. Such permanent structures affect who interrelates with whom and for how long. They also determine how you may perceive and structure your informal space.

In semi-fixed space, the environments physical features are partially changeable. For example, furnishings can be rearranged for different effects. Such semi-permanent arrangements permit a variety of spaces in which to conduct communication activities. Combined, the fixed, semi-fixed, and informal spaces create a total space structure for each of us that communicate to us and determines the type of communication activities in which we engage.

Most scholars in the field of proxemics also study how groups use space. The way people in groups allocate their assigned spaces determines the group leader, favourite members, types of interaction pattern, and such. For example, contrast five people seated in a straight row at a table with the same five seated at a round table. You will definitely find a different pattern of interaction between the two. Also, you will find different immediate leaders and conversation topics. People who begin conversations and people who are seated at the ends are usually considered leaders, at least at first. Obviously, space patterns can be rearranged to achieve different results. If possible, you should use space to accomplish a particular purpose. This usage is especially important if you are a manager and thus the one responsible for the outcome.

(C) The Language

Another type of non-verbal communication, time language involves the meaning we give to time, that is how we communicate to others what times means to us. In order to give meaning to time, we must perceive it, filter it, and symbolise about it. But our final symbolising about time is not always done with word.

We attempt to control time, trying to become much more efficient in our use of it. Most of us look to our cultures to get meaning for time. We are taught that the future is important, how we use our time in our personal and professional schedules reflects how our culture has taught us to perceive time. Try being late for an appointment and see how others respond. Generally, when someone is late, we react negatively; when someone arrives early, we see him or her as eager or aggressive. Agendas used at meetings are designed to keep us on time. Businesses generally pay employees more for working overtime, weekends and holidays. You can conclude from these examples, that we communicate our ideas about time with our non-verbal behaviours, both personally and professionally.

As a communicator, you should recognise the receivers time language. You must remember that not all time perspectives are the same. You should also be aware that you have a time language uniquely your own. It projects your own meanings for time. Finally, you can and should adapt time meaning to fit the receiver's mind just as you do your words in written or spoken messages.

(D) Paralanguage

Still another types of non-verbal communication is known as paralanguage or paralinguistic. Of all the non-verbal types, it is the closest to actual verbal communication. By paralanguage, we mean how a person says something. Paralanguage involves the "how" of a speaker's voice rather than the words. Para means like, thus, paralanguage literally means "like language". It involves those hints and signals in a person's voice that gives us meaning.

In paralanguage, we examine the sound of someone's speech. Is it fast or slow? Is it high pitched or deep? Is it loud and forceful or barely audible? Is it smooth or disjointed? These are the types of signals with which paralanguage is concerned. The signals (as symbols) become a part of the total meaning one receives. For example, read the following series of statements, emphasising the underlined word in each;

1 practice good business communication.

I practice good business communication.

I practice good business communication.

I practice good business communication.

I practice good business communication.

By concentrating on the underlined word, you give different meanings to each statement even though the same words are used. As still another example, try counting from one to ten to express various emotional states - say, nervousness, happiness, and anger. The way in which you express each sequence will tell the receiver what you intend quite accurately.

The preceding examples are designed to illustrate that the way, in which one delivers a message, communicates. A person's voice, tone and quality may or may not be consistent with the meaning attached to the actual words. What you need for effective communication is consistency. Also, you should realise that there are various things you can do to change the meaning of your oral message. Paralanguage includes pauses and insertions, such as "oh", "uh", "you know", and the like, since these signal our meanings too.

As a sender, you should particularly avoid sending "mixed signals "-saying one thing in one way and using words that intend the opposite". As far as possible, you should make what and the how of your message blend. As a receiver, you should concentrate on both how the message is sent and the meaning of the words Look for consistencies and inconsistencies. Indeed, the spcken words can tell you much about the entire message's intended meaning if you listen carefully between the lines.

(E) Physical Context

We get meaning from our surroundings. The surroundings provide cues in our sensory environment. We get messages from these cues through the meaning we give to colour and to the layout/ design of the parts of our physical environment.

Colour: Most people who study the effects of colours conclude that different colours are associated with different moods and behaviours. Artists, interior decorators, and "image" consultants all contend that the right colour combinations can project appropriate feelings. It would appear, then, that we have a "colour language" in addition to the other types of languages we have mentioned. Technically, of course, we do not see colour; rather, we see light waves, which create colour associations within us that we have learned. Nevertheless, we will consider some basic ideas about colour as part of our physical context.

Research on the effects of colours is far from complete. Yet we can confirm that the colours of our clothing, office interiors, and the like do make an impression. Moreover, we receive meanings from colours we perceive. Rather than giving any colour selection casual attention, we should devote more thought to colour coordination, particularly when doing so will help us achieve a desired effect. In addition, we should consider lighting, sound and other contextual features with equal attentiveness.

Layout and design: Another meaningful part of our physical context is the layout and design of our surroundings. The space arrangements of an office, the presence or absence of carpeting, the layout of the desk and chairs and office size all tell someone something about us. To test the reality of this component of context, try taking a part of the layout/design away and see another person's reaction. Or rearrange parts of the environment without telling another person and look for the negative reaction you will likely get.

The importance of layout and design is evident from the volumes written by architects, industrial engineers and production researchers on the subject. The layout and design of our surroundings communicate things about us to others. Perhaps they convey our status in a group or perhaps our needs for formality. In whatever non-verbal ways layout and design communicate, we should be aware of them so that we can use this part of our surroundings to contribute effectively to the success of our communication efforts.

One of the first things we can conclude about non-verbal communication is its commonness. If you look around you for just a moment, you will see all types of non-verbal communication. The key to detecting these non-verbal aspects of communication, however, lies in learning how to look for them. While this is so, we are probably unaware of their extent. Put differently, we are more conscious of our verbal communication, but once we learn about the non-verbal aspects, we can be conscious of them as well. Then we can look for their combined meaning in a communication situation.

Non-verbal communication is that its symbols are vague and inconsistent. Often non-verbal symbols are supplements to verbal communications used without conscious intent. Sometimes they enhance and sometimes they alter the intended meaning. Thus, for best communication results, we must look carefully at the non-verbal symbols we perceive. We must use our best judgment to determine the sender's intended meanings.

We could analyse written communication for its non-verbal parts, non-verbal communication applies primarily to face-to-face, oral communication because this is where we can most readily observe the non-verbal symbols.

3.14.2 Using Effectively Non-verbal Communication

"The most important thing in communication is to hear what isn't being said." - Peter F. Drucker

"Spoken language is only 7 per cent to 35 per cent of communication. The majority of our feelings and intentions are sent through nonverbal communication. Moreover we tend to search for signals when verbal messages are unclear or ambiguous. Wordless messages or kinesics are the way we communicate by sending and receiving signals using body language, gestures, postures, proximity, hepatics, and facial expressions. Some signals are consistent across cultures. To a certain degree this is good news; if you do not speak the foreign language, you can still communicate with people of another country by using body language and facial expressions. However, even if you do speak the local language and are able to communicate with the local people you might still be puzzled by the use of body language and facial expressions at your destination country.

Why?

Because nonverbal communication has also cultural meanings and is being interpreted according to the cultural context it occurs. Cultural norms regarding kinesics vary considerably between countries; if you are not familiar with the local body language you might be misunderstood, and sometimes misinterpret the local non-verbal signals. This can certainly lead to embarrassing and uncomfortable situations. It is recommended to obtain as much information as you can about the non-verbal communication codes that are customary at a country. Understanding body language correctly and interpreting it accordingly assist you to avoid unpleasant situation but will grant you respect from the locals.

Good communication is the foundation of successful relationships, both personally and professionally. But we communicate with body language much more than words. In fact, research shows that the majority of our communication is non-verbal. Non-verbal communication, or *body language*, includes our facial expressions, gestures, eye contact, posture, and even the tone of our voice.

The ability to understand and use nonverbal communication is powerful tools that will help you connect with others, express what you really mean, navigate challenging situations, and build better relationship.

Non-verbal communication, or body language, is a vital form of communication. When we interact with others, we continuously give and receive countless wordless signals. All of our non-verbal behaviours - the gestures we make, the way we sit, how fast or how loud we talk, how close we stand, how much eye contact we make send strong messages. The way you listen, look, move, and react tell the other person whether or not you care and how well you're listening. The non-verbal signals you send either produce a sense of interest, trust, and desire for connection or they generate disinterest, distrust, and confusion.

Non-verbal Communication Cues can Play Five Roles:

- *Repetition*: they can repeat the message the person is making verbally.

- *Contradiction*: they can contradict a message the individual is trying to convey.

- *Substitution*: they can substitute for a verbal message. For example, a person's eyes can often convey a far more vivid message than words and often do.

- *Complementing*: they may add to or complement a verbal message. A boss who pats a person on the back in addition to giving praise can increase the impact of the message.

- *Accenting*: they may accent or underline a verbal message. Pounding the table, for example, can underline a message.

It takes more than words to create fulfilling, strong relationships. Non-verbal communication has a huge impact on the quality of our relationships. Non-verbal communication skills improve relationships by helping you:

- Accurately read other people, including the emotions they're feeling and the unspoken messages they're sending.

- Create trust and transparency in relationships by sending non-verbal signals that match up with your words.

- Respond with non-verbal cues that show others that you understand, notice, and care.

Unfortunately, many people send confusing or negative non-verbal signals without even knowing it. When this happens, both connection and trust are lost in our relationships.

It's not what you say, it's how you say it

- *Intensity*. A reflection of the amount of energy you project is considered your intensity. Again, this has as much to do with what feels good to the other person as what you personally prefer.

- *Timing and pace*. Your ability to be a good listener and communicate interest and involvement is impacted by timing and pace.

Sounds that convey understanding. Sounds such as "ahhh, ummm, ohhh," uttered with congruent eye and facial gestures, communicate understanding and emotional connection. More than words, these sounds are the language of interest, understanding and concern.

Using body language and non-verbal communication successfully

Nonverbal communication is a rapidly flowing back-and-forth process. Successful non-verbal communication depends on emotional self-awareness and an understanding of the cues you're sending, along with the ability to accurately pick up on the cues others are sending you. This requires your full concentration and attention. If you are planning what you're going to say next, daydreaming, or thinking about something else, you are almost certain to miss nonverbal cues and other detail in the conversation. You need to stay focused on the moment-to-moment experience in order to fully understand what's going on.

Tips for Successful Non-verbal Communication

- Take a time out if you're feeling overwhelmed by stress. Stress compromises your ability to communicate. When you're stressed out, you're more likely to misread other people, send off confusing or off-putting non-verbal signals, and lapse into unhealthy knee-jerk patterns of behaviour. Take a moment to calm down before you jump back into the conversation. Once you've regained your emotional equilibrium, you'll be better equipped to deal with the situation in a positive way.

- Pay attention to inconsistencies. Non-verbal communication should reinforce what is being said. If you get the feeling that someone isn't being honest or that something is "off," you may be picking up on a mismatch between verbal and non-verbal cues. Is the person is saying one thing, and their body language something else? For example, are they telling you "yes" while shaking their head "no"?

- Look at non-verbal communication signals as a group. Don't read too much into a single gesture or non-verbal cue. Consider all of the non-verbal signals you are sending and receiving, from eye contact to tone of voice and body language. Are your non-verbal cues consistent or inconsistent with what you are trying to communicate?

Improving Your Non-verbal Communication Skills

Before you can improve your non-verbal communication skills, you need to figure out what you're doing right and where there is room for improvement. The most effective method is to observe yourself in action:

- *Video camera* – Videotape a conversation between you and a partner. Set the camera to record both of you at the same time, so you can observe the non-verbal back-and-forth. When you watch the recording, focus on any discrepancies between your verbal and non-verbal communication.

- *Digital camera* – Ask someone to take a series of photos of you while you're talking to someone else. As you look through the photos, focus on you and the other person's body language, facial expressions, and gestures.

- *Audio recorder* – Record a conversation between you and a friend or family member. As you listen to the recording afterwards, concentrate on the way things are said, rather than the words. Pay attention to tone, timing, pace, and other sounds.

As you watch or listen to the recordings, ask yourself the following questions:

- **Eye contact** - Is this source of connection missing, too intense, or just right in yourself or in the person you are looking at?

- **Facial expression** - What is your face showing? Is it mask-like and unexpressive, or emotionally present and filled with interest? What do you see as you look into the faces of others?

- **Tone of voice** - Does your voice project warmth, confidence, and delight, or is it strained and blocked? What do you hear as you listen to other people?

- **Posture and gesture** - Does your body look still and immobile, or relaxed? Sensing the degree of tension in your shoulders and jaw answers this question. What do you observe about the degree of tension or relaxation in the body of the person you are speaking to?

- **Touch** - Remember, what feels good is relative. How do you like to be touched? Who do you like to have touching you? Is the difference between what you like and what the other person likes obvious to you?

- **Intensity** - Do you or the person you are communicating with seem flat, cool, and disinterested, or over-the-top and melodramatic? Again, this has as much to do with what feels good to the other person as it does with what you personally prefer.

- **Timing and pace** - What happens when you or someone you care about makes an important statement? Does a response—

not necessarily verbal—come too quickly or too slowly? Is there an easy flow of information back and forth?

- **Sounds** - Do you use sounds to indicate that you are attending to the other person? Do you pick up on sounds from others?

3.14.3 Body Language

Have you ever been in the situation when you really didn't believe what someone was saying? Did you have a sense that something didn't ring true or a gut feeling that all was not right? Perhaps they were saying 'Yes' yet their heads were shaking 'No'? The difference between the words people speak and our understanding of what they are saying comes from non-verbal communication, otherwise known as "body language". By developing your awareness of the signs and signals of body language, you can more easily understand other people, and more effectively communicate with them.

There are sometimes slight - and sometimes visible - movements, gestures, facial expressions and even shifts in our whole bodies that indicate something is going on. The way we talk, walk, sit and stand all say something about us, and whatever is happening on the inside can be reflected on the outside. By becoming more aware of this body language and understanding what it might mean, you can learn to read people more easily. This puts you in a better position to communicate effectively with them. What's more, by increasing your understanding of others, you can also become more aware of the messages that you convey to them. There are times when we send mixed messages - we say one thing yet our body language reveals something different. This non-verbal language will affect how we act and react to others, and how they react to us.

First Impressions and Confidence

Recall a time when you met someone new at work. Or think about the last time you watched a speaker delivering a presentation. What were your first impressions? Did you sense confidence or a lack of confidence in them? Did you want to associate with them or not? Did they convince you? Did they stride into the room, engage you and maintain eye contact or were they tentative, shuffling towards you with eyes averted, before sliding into a chair? What about their handshake – firm and strong or weak and limp? Moving along in the conversation, did they maintain solid eye contact or were they frequently looking away? Did their face appear relaxed or was it tight and tense? What about their hand and arm movements? Were their gestures wide, flowing and open or were they tight, jerky and closed?

As you observe others, you can identify some common signs and signals that give away whether they are feeling confident or not. Typical things to look for in confident people include:

- *Posture* – standing tall with shoulders back.
- *Eye contact* – solid with a 'smiling' face.
- *Gestures with hands and arms* – purposeful and deliberate.
- *Speech* – slow and clear.
- *Tone of voice* – moderate to low.

As well as decoding other people's body language, you can use this knowledge to convey feelings that you're not actually experiencing. For example, if you are about to enter into a situation where you are not as confident as you'd like to be, such as giving a big presentation or attending an important meeting, you can adopt these 'confidence' signs and signals to project confidence. Let's now look at another scenario.

Difficult Meetings and Defensiveness

Think of a time when you were in a difficult meeting – perhaps a performance appraisal or one where you are negotiating deadlines, responsibilities or a contract. In an ideal world, both you and the other person would be open and receptive to hearing what each other has to say, in order to conclude the meeting successfully.

However, often, the other person is defensive and doesn't really listen. If this happens during an appraisal meeting, and it's important for you to convey to your colleague that he or she needs to change certain behaviours, you really want them open and receptive to you so they take on board what you are saying. So how can you tell whether your message is falling on "deaf ears"?

Some of the common signs that the person you are speaking with may be feeling defensive include:

- Hand/arm gestures are small and close to his or her body.
- Facial expressions are minimal.
- Body is physically turned away from you.
- Arms are crossed in front of body.
- Eyes maintain little contact, or are downcast.

By picking up these signs, you can change what you say or how you say it to help the other person become more at ease, and more receptive to what you are saying. Equally, if you are feeling somewhat defensive going into a negotiating situation, you can monitor your own body language to ensure that the messages you are conveying are ones that say that you are open and receptive to what is being discussed.

Working with Groups and Disengagement

Have you ever delivered a presentation, and had a sense that people weren't really buying into what you had to say? What about working with a group to facilitate a consensus on responsibilities and deadlines? Was everyone on board with the ideas, or did some appear disengaged?

Ideally, when you stand up to deliver a presentation or work with group, you want 100 per cent engagement with all concerned. This often doesn't happen on its own, though. But you can actively engage the audience when you need to if you're alert to some of the typical signs and signals of people not being engaged. Some of these signs and signals include:

- Heads are down.

- Eyes are glazed, or gazing at something else.
- Hands may be picking at cloths, or fiddling with pens.
- People may be writing or doodling.
- They may be sitting slumped in their chairs.

When you pick up that someone appears not to be engaged in what is going on, you can do something to re-engage him or her and bring their focus back to what you are saying, such as asking them a direct question. And while this is going on, make sure that your own body language is saying what you want it to.

Lying

Of all the non-verbal body language that we may observe, being able to tell whether a person is lying or not will stand you in good stead. Some of the typical signs and signals that a person is lying include:

- Eyes maintain little or no eye contact, or there may be rapid eye movements, with pupils constricted.
- Hand or fingers are in front of his or her mouth when speaking.
- His or her body is physically turned away from you, or there are un-usual/un-natural body gestures.
- His or her breathing rate increases.
- Complexion changes such as in colour; red in face or neck area.
- Perspiration increases.
- Voice changes such as change in pitch, stammering, throat clearing.

As with all non-verbal language, it's important to remember here that everyone's personal body language is slightly different.

If you notice some of the typical non-verbal signs of lying, you shouldn't necessarily jump to conclusions, as many of these signals can be confused with the appearance of nervousness. What you should do, however, is use these signals as a prompt to probe further, ask more questions and explore the area in more detail to determine whether they are being truthful or not. Further clarification is always worthwhile when checking out your understanding of someone's body language, and this is particularly true during job interviews and in negotiating situations.

3.14.4 Non-verbal Cues

Most communication is not verbal. Even when you are not speaking, you are still communicating non-verbally.

In the communication process, you affect other team members and they affect you without saying a word. You send positive and negative messages by the way you communicate non-verbally.

The following table contains several non-verbal actions and their perceived meanings :

Non-verbal response	*What it may indicate?*
Bouncing your leg	Impatience; Urgency; Lack of interest
Raising your eyebrow	Disbelief; Questioning; Surprise
Nodding your head	Approval; Encouragement; Understanding
Leaning forward	Interest; Concentration; Care
Remaining silent	Concentration; Interest; Respect
Frowning	Disapproval; Sadness; Lack of understanding
Looking away	Distraction; Impatience; Lack of interest
Rolling your eyes	Disapproval; Disbelief; Lack of understanding
Restlessness	Lack of interest; Message too lengthy; Discomfort

In a team or small group, you have many opportunities to send or respond to non-verbal messages. For example, if your team members are giving you non-verbal cues that they do not understand or accept your message, you can respond by clarifying it or by changing your approach.

3.15 Verbal Communication

The basis of communication is the interaction between people. Verbal communication is one way for people to communicate face-to-face. Some of the key components of verbal communication are sound, words, speaking, and language. At birth, most people have vocal cords, which produce sounds. As a child grows it learns how to form these sounds into words. Some words may be imitative of natural sounds, but others may come from expressions of emotion, such as laughter or crying. Words alone have no meaning. Only people can put meaning into words. As meaning is assigned to words, language develops, which leads to the development of speaking.

The actual origin of language is subject to considerable speculation. Some theorists believe it is an outgrowth of group activities such as working together or dancing. Others believe that language developed from basic sounds and gestures. Over 3,000 languages and major dialects are spoken in the world today. The development of languages reflects class, gender, profession, age group, and other social factors. The huge variety of languages usually creates difficulties between different languages, but even within a single language there can be many problems in understanding.

Through speaking we try to eliminate this misunderstanding, but sometimes this is a very hard thing to do. Just as we assume that our messages are clearly received, so we assume that because something is important to us, it is important to others. As time has proven this is not at all true. Many problems can arise in speaking and the only way to solve these problems is through experience. Speaking can be looked at in two major areas: interpersonal and public speaking. Since the majority of speaking is an interpersonal process, to communicate effectively we must not simply clean up our language, but learn to relate to people.

In interpersonal speaking, etiquette is very important. To be an effective communicator one must speak in a manner that is not offending to the receiver. Etiquette also plays an important role in an area that has developed in most all business settings:

hierarchical communication. In business today, hierarchical communication is of utmost importance to all members involved. The other major area of speaking is public speaking. From the origin of time, it has been obvious that some people are just better public speakers than others. Because of this, today a good speaker can earn a living by speaking to people in a public setting. Some of the major areas of public speaking are speaking to persuade, speaking to inform, and speaking to inspire or motivate.

Interpersonal Speaking

Verbal communication is an essential part of business and when it is executed correctly, good things happen. Here are a few different ideas and styles to remember when speaking to anyone in a business setting. Because speaking is such an indelible activity, we tend to do it without much thought. But, that casual approach can be a problem in business. Have you ever wished you could make a second, first impression because you said something that was out of character or embarrassing? That comment that you didn't think about before you said, has created an image in someone's mind that cannot be replaced even when you meant something totally different. When it comes to oral communication, your goal should be to take advantage of its positive characteristics while minimising the dangers. Speaking can be used as a tool to accomplish your objectives. But, first you must break the habit of talking spontaneously without planning what you're going to say or how you're going to say it. You must learn to manage the impression you create by consciously tailoring your remarks and delivery style to suit the situation. Here are some things, which will make you an effective communicator:

- Remember to become aware of what you are saying.
- Apply the same process you use in written communication when you are communicating orally.
- Before you speak, think about your purpose, your main idea, and your audience.
- Organise your thoughts in a logical way.

- Decide on a style that suits the occasion and then edit your remarks mentally.
- As you speak, watch the other person to see whether your message is making the desired impression. If not, revise it and try again.

Remember that various situations call for different speaking styles, just as various writing assignments call for different writing styles. Here are four different styles that will suit every occasion:

- *Expressive style* is spontaneous, conversational, and natural. Use this when you are expressing your feelings, joking, complaining, or socialising.
- *Directive style* is an authoritative and judgmental style. We use this style to give orders, exert leadership, pass judgment, or state our opinions.
- *Problem-solving style* is rational, objective, unbiased, and bland. This is the style most commonly used in business dealings. We use it when we are solving problems and conveying routine information.
- *Meta style* is used to discuss the communication process itself. Meta language enables us to talk about our interactions.

Following these few helpful tips will increase your communication awareness, which will ultimately increase your value as an employee.

Hierarchical Communication

People communicate in businesses with each other most often by oral communication. This talking takes place between managers, coworkers and subordinates alike. In organisations, communication skill is used to send messages 64 per cent of the time. That is why it is important to understand all the concept of communication.

Have you ever noticed how people communicate differently to their bosses than they would communicate to their coworkers?

This difference in communication is due to the chain of command. Managers or "bosses" are typically in an influential position over their employees. Managers have authority or the right to give orders and expect the orders to be obeyed. Many employees may feel that any bad attitude or disagreement with their superior may result in a bad relationship with the boss and therefore create a bad work environment or job description.

In most cases employees talk to their coworkers in a friendly manner. The overall standard is that workers will speak more freely and openly to their fellow workers than to their superiors. When workers talk to each other and relay information on to other workers it is called the "grapevine". The grapevine is the unofficial way that communication takes place in an organisation. It is neither authorised nor supported by the organisation. Information is spread by word or mouth and even through electronic means today. The grapevine can be used by an "open" company and it will have accurate information however, in an authoritative culture the rumor mill may not be accurate.

Communication from a manager to a subordinate is also different. One reason for this may be because of the arising concern by managers not to offend their workers or say the wrong thing. In today's society, lawsuits run rapid over conversations that some employees may take offensive from their bosses. Managers have a responsibility to know and follow guidelines of good business communication etiquette.

The last type of difference in communication is between the male and female sexes. It was found that when men talk, they do so to emphasise status and independence. Women are found to talk to create connections and intimacy. Women speak about a problem as a means of promoting closeness and to gain support and connection while men talk to solve a problem or give advice.

Etiquette

In today's competitive business environment, social skills and proper etiquette can mean the difference between finding and winning the job of your career and standing still in your career.

The confidence of knowing you can hold your own in any social setting, from the white-knuckled nervousness of a first interview to a casual business lunch, can change the way people perceive and judge you. The key to proper business etiquette is: "Do unto others as they would want you to do unto them."

To be successful in the business world, a person must use proper verbal etiquette. One important aspect of verbal etiquette is a proper introduction. Every day we encounter people in a variety of business and social situations. The way we meet and greet them creates lasting impressions and paves the way for a productive encounter. Introductions project information. Besides the obvious elements of name, title, and affiliation, an introduction conveys a level of respect and reflects how the person making the introduction views the other person's status. Mastering the art of the introduction will help put you and the people you are introducing at ease. Learning the basics - and they are not very difficult - is the first step.

Basic points to remember when making introductions:

- The most important point about introductions is to always make them, even if you can't remember names. Failing to do so causes embarrassment and discomfort. If given a choice, most people would prefer you to make the introduction incorrectly, even if you forgot their name, rather than stand there unacknowledged and disregarded.

- A second important point in any introduction is the order of names. The name of the person being introduced is mentioned last, and the person to whom the introduction is made is mentioned first. In a business setting, introductions are based on power and hierarchy. Simply, persons of lesser authority are introduced to persons of greater authority. Gender plays no role in business etiquette; nor does it affect the order of introductions.

Another important aspect of verbal etiquette is the way in which people address others in a business setting. Once introduced, improperly addressing superiors, colleagues, customers and clients, or subordinates at future meetings may create tension and will create a negative impression. Generally, it is appropriate to address subordinates and others with whom an informal relationship has been established by their first name. In formal relationships, or when the relationship status is unknown, it is necessary to refer to the individual using the appropriate gender-specific title. When gender-specific titles are necessary, use Mister (Mr.) to address men, Misses (Mrs.) to address married women, and Miss (Ms.) to address women who are single or whose marital status is unknown. Following are more specific rules for addressing others in business settings:

- *Superiors*: Always address superiors with the appropriate gender-specific title, unless he/she gives express permission to do otherwise.

- *Colleagues*: It is generally accepted procedure to address colleagues by first name. Exceptions arise when the relationship is formal or unfamiliar.

- *Subordinates*: If the superior has established an informal relationship with the subordinate, use of first names is appropriate. If the relationship is formal or unfamiliar, the appropriate gender-specific title is necessary.

- *Clients and Customers*: Most relationships with clients or customers are formal, dictating appropriate gender-specific titles. Occasionally, though, an amiable relationship has been established and would allow the use of first names.

A third aspect of business etiquette is proper telephone procedure. Since much of today's business is done over the phone, using correct telephone etiquette is more important than ever. Lasting impressions may be formed during and after telephone conversations, and business people, in order to be successful, must maintain a positive impression. This dictates that people use proper telephone etiquette.

3.15.1 The Psychology of Verbal Communication

Communication occurs when signals carry information-bearing messages between a source (or sender) and a destination (or receiver).

Although all species communicate, human communication is notable for its precision and flexibility a consequence of the uniquely human ability to use language. Language endows human communication system with the properties of semanticity, generativity, and displacement, allowing people to formulate an unlimited number of meaningful novel messages that are not tied to the immediate present. At a fundamental level verbal message convey meanings the speaker has encoded into the words of an utterance, but a listener who has understood the utterance has gone beyond the literal meaning of the words and grasped the particular sense in which the speaker intended them to be understood. In order to do so, communicators must make their co-participants perspectives part of the process of formulating and interpreting messages. Thus, any communicative exchange is implicitly a joint or collective activity in which meaning emerges from the participants' collaborative efforts.

Although linguists think about language as an abstract structure—a set of principles that specify the relations between a sequence of sounds and a sequence of meanings—to its users, what is most significant about language is its versatility as a medium for communication. The ability to communicate is vital to a species' survival, and all animal species communicate, some in ways that are impressively proficient. But none achieve the precision and flexibility that characterises human communication, a capacity due in large part to the uniquely human ability to use language.

Semanticity, Generativity, and Displacement

Language is only one of the symbol systems humans use to communicate. The "thumbs-up" gesture conveys the message of success, approval or hope; the wedding ring and the mourner's ribbon publicly proclaim the wearer's current status; a facial grimace in response to the question "How did you like the movie?" symbolically and effectively expresses the person's assessment. Notwithstanding the utility of such symbolic displays, language endows human communication with three properties, semanticity, generativity, and displacement that collectively distinguish it from other sorts of symbolic displays and from the forms of communication observed in other species.

- **Semanticity:** In human communication, signals stand for things, which is to say that they have meaning.

- **Generativity (sometimes called Productivity):** All languages are capable of generating an infinite number of meaningful messages from a finite number of linguistic signals. Languages allow symbols to be combined and recombined in ways that yield novel meanings, and any competent language user will regularly produce and comprehend utterances that have never been uttered before, but are immediately comprehensible to all competent language users.

- **Displacement:** Language makes it possible to communicate about things that are remote in space or time, or indeed exist only in the imagination. Although the observation is self-evident, it points to a fundamental difference in the expressive capacities of language and other communication modalities. The ability of language to generate an unlimited number of meaningful novel messages that are not bound to the here and now, combined with the cognitive capacity to exploit these properties, allows human communication to be extraordinarily effective and versatile. The full extent of this effectiveness and versatility is revealed by an examination of how communication systems work. Regardless of the type of signal, all communication involves the transfer of information between a source and a destination.

3.15.2 Managerial Work and Communication

Managers work in a stimulus-reactive environment. The nature of their work is typically varied, spasmodic and brief, and they do a great quantity of work at an unrelenting pace. In general, they prefer to deal with specific issues, prefer verbal media, and to control to some degree their own activities. However, it is likely that managers will carry out their work, even in very similar jobs, in different ways, dependent on their choices concerning what to do and how to do it. These choices are influenced by the managers own perceptions, preferences and personal characteristics.

Within their personal work contexts, managers work in three clearly identifiable roles, which change rapidly from one to another because of the episodic nature of their work. These roles can be classified as interpersonal, informational and decisional. However, to make effective decisions (allocating resources, dealing with problems, etc.) managers need to collect relevant information, and to collect information they require effective formal and informal communication with bosses, colleagues (often in other functions), subordinates, and contacts external to the organisation. So, to be effective managers, skilled in decision making (on which they are most frequently judged and appraised for salary and promotion), they need to be effective communicators. But as they make choices regarding their approach to individual jobs, the specific communication skills they need will vary from manager to manager, from job to job.

3.15.3 Managers and Communication

One of the classic managerial dilemma that of balancing the pressure of short-term results with the need to take a long-term view, as in problem solving and making decisions versus planning, forecasting, etc. Managers have to work within the political reality of their organisations and to recognise that they need to build power bases in order to influence others. This means that they have to (a) develop credibility for their personal and professional expertise and (b) be able to communicate with and influence other managers. When you consider the nature and purposes of the communication that managers have to carry out, the topic takes on whole new dimensions. The audience might be public or private, requiring adjustments of style. Among the numerous purposes of communication, some are as follows:

- Seeking or receiving information, allocating blame, encouragement, control, selling proposals, confrontation. Talking to different levels within the hierarchy - to individuals, to groups, to departments - and externally to customers, suppliers, banks, other professionals.

- Using formal communication, meetings, reports, proposals, notices; and informal communication: counseling, advising, and talking to other employees.

- Working in different roles: as chairman, project leader, analyst, subordinate and colleague.

- Evaluating communications: are they facts, opinions, gossip.
- Building up networks to obtain real information which may be given freely or concealed - which means you need to ask the right questions, or else you will find yourself drowned in data but starved of information.
- Trying to influence those over whom you have no power.
- Managers need to be effective communicators to achieve positive results in today's organisations.

3.15.4 Management Style and Communication

As a manager, you try to get things done through other people. This means you manage people and the resources you require to get the task done. The management of people can be called leadership, and all of us have our own preferred leadership styles, which affect the ways in which we communicate with others, especially our staff. There is however, no one magic style, which will make us effective leaders. We have to work at it, to develop different styles, which are most appropriate to the three elements in every leadership situations.

- You, the leader
- Your staff
- The task to be done.

Only by understanding and analyzing these three elements can you choose the right style for any given situation. There are four leadership styles (see Fig. 3.4):

- Directing
- Coaching
- Supporting
- Delegating

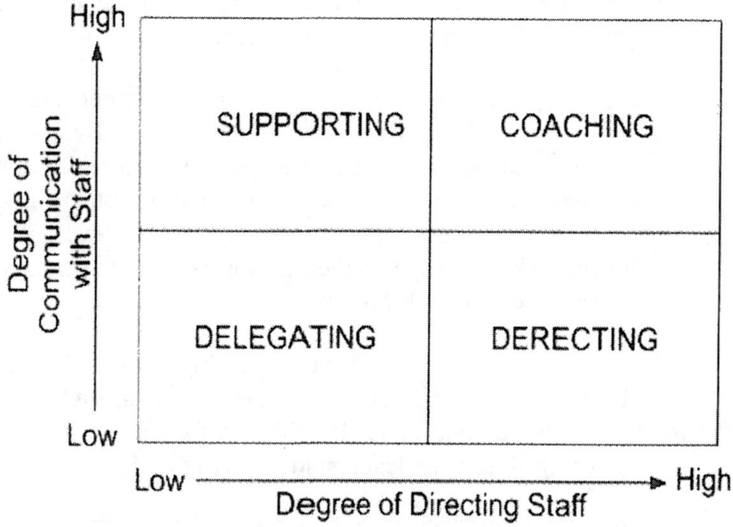

Fig. 3.4. Four Basic Leadership Styles.

Each of these is appropriate, in the right situation (but we will have our preferred style and often find it difficult to change that style even when we need to).

- **Directing** is most appropriate when a complex task has to be performed and your staff is not experienced or motivated to do it; or when you are under time pressure for completion. You explain what needs to be done, and tell them what to do. In such a situation, you can fall into the trap of over-communicating: excessive explanation can confuse and waste time.

- **Coaching** is appropriate when your people are more motivated and are becoming more experienced in coping with the task. Here you would explain in more detail and help them to understand by spending time building up a good relationship with them.

- **Supporting** works when people are familiar with the techniques required and have further developed their relationship with you. You take time to talk to them, to involve them more in work decisions, to listen to their suggestions for improving performance.

- **Delegating** is right when your staff is thoroughly conversant and efficient in the performance of the task, and you can simply let them get on with it. People of experience do not take kindly to a manager sitting on their shoulders and interfering with every aspect of their work. However, you still need to keep an eye on their performance to ensure that your required standards are maintained.

If you combine the four basic leadership styles with the characteristics and the experience of the people you are which is the most appropriate style of leadership in a particular situation you will be using situational leadership (see Fig. 3.5).

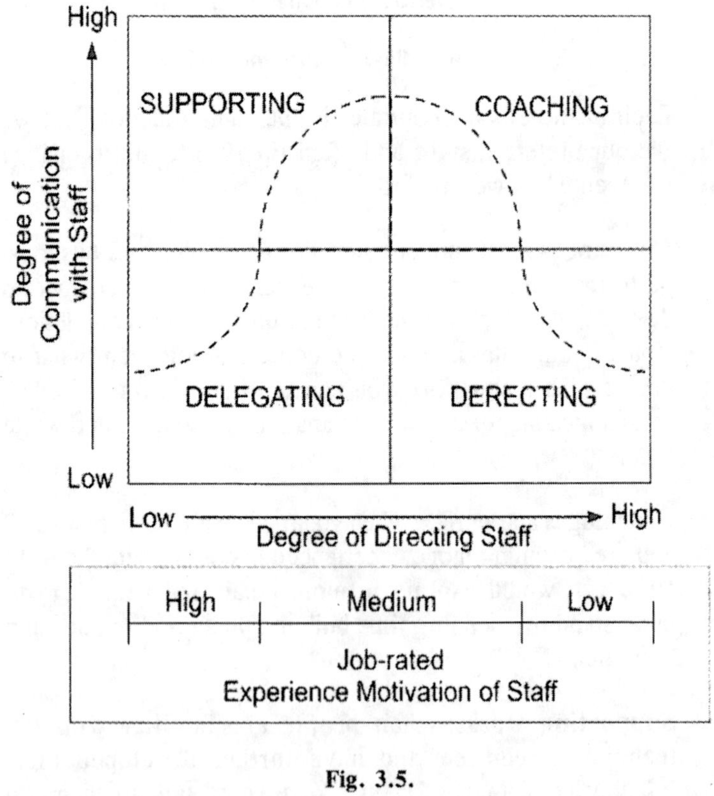

Fig. 3.5.

To become effective in choosing the right style of leadership in other words to change your style to meet the needs of situation – you need to develop three specific skills.

- *Analytical skills*: to access the degree of experience and motivation your subordinates bring to the achievement of the task
- *Flexibility skills*: to vary your style of leadership to the most appropriate one based on your analysis of the situation.
- *Communication skill*: to explain why you are varying your leadership style in different situation to the individuals, subordinates concerned. Each person's experience and motivation to perform certain task will be different. People whom you might usually manage in a delegating style would reach adversely to a directing style if you are not capable of communicating effectively to them that the reason you are using a different style is that the task you are asking them to perform is of a nature which is completely unfamiliar to them.

Most people whom you manage are likely to fall into the medium experience, medium motivation categories. So the two styles - supporting, and coaching - will work for you most of the time. But, if you stick to these styles, to paraphrase Abraham Lincoln, "you can manage 80 per cent of your people effectively for 100 per cent of the time, or 100 per cent of your people for 80 per cent of the time, but you can't manage 100 per cent of your people effectively for 100 per cent of the time". You will need to use all your styles at some time or another, and so you will need to develop the following communication skills:

- How to explain clearly, and concisely, the nature of the task.
- How to tell people what to do and how to do it.
- How to encourage people when work is well done.
- How to build relationships with your staff.
- How to share problems with them, and listen to their ideas and feelings?

- How to delegate effectively, so that there is a clear understanding?

- What problems people should bring to you?

- How to explain why you are behaving differently as a leader in a particular situation - why, in effect, you are being consistent in your inconsistency.

3.15.5 Improving Verbal Skills

Communication Methods
Speaking, Listening
Distortion in Sending and Receiving Messages
Listening skills - a key to effective communication
Improving Presentation Skills
Leadership Communications Skills

Experts say that communication is composed of different methods: words, voice, tone and non-verbal clues. Of these, some are more effective in delivering a message than others. According to research, in a conversation or verbal exchange:

- Words are seven per cent effective

- Tone of voice is 38 per cent effective

- Non-verbal clues are 55 per cent effective

- Non-verbal clues include:

- Body language (e.g., arms crossed, standing, sitting, relaxed, tense).

- Emotion of the sender and receiver (e.g., yelling, speaking provocatively, enthusiastic).

- Other connections between the people (e.g., friends, enemies, professional similarities or differences, personal similarities or differences, age similarities or differences, philosophical similarities or differences, attitudes, expectations).

In other words, WHAT you say is not nearly as important as HOW you say it! A dull message delivered by a charming person, filled with energy and enthusiasm will be accepted as brilliant. An excellent message delivered by someone who is not interested in the topic, will not engage the enthusiasm of its intended audience.

3.16 Summary

Effective communication in organisation, like effective communication anywhere, involves getting accurate message from one person to another or to several people. There are several factors that affect the effectiveness of communication in an organisation, like organisations authority, job specialisation, information ownership, communications channels etc. Organisations design their own communication networks for the desired flow of information's.

Communication may be one or two way. Though thé two-way communication takes more time than one-way communication, it has the advantage of being more accurate and yet in an organisation, because of its orderliness, economical and efficient, the one-way communication has no less importance. The effective superior-subordinate communication achieves the purpose of giving specific job instructions, directions, organisational procedures, etc. Each organisation has several departments. Communication between departments seeks to enrich the lives of individual throughout the organisation by reducing misunderstanding, avoiding analogonisms, encouraging co-operation and promoting sincerity.

One of the greatest challenges that the managers in organisation have to face are how to get on with the people and even get over them for getting the work done, so interpersonal communication skill assumes greater significance. In order to ensure the communication effectiveness in the organisation various modes of communication are used, viz. Conversation, Speeches, Presentations, Dictations, Telephones, Interviews, Discussions, Teleconferencing, Memo, Reports, and Proposals etc. Each mode accomplishes specific objectives and has its own advantages and disadvantages.

All communications that involve neither written nor spoken words but occur without the use of words are the Non-verbal communications. The body communicates through its physical movements. Facial expressions are associated with happiness, surprise, fear, anger and sadness. The eyes along with eyebrows, upper and lower eyelids, size of pupils, convey certain body inner states. In addition to face and eye, physical movements of arms, legs, hands, head also convey meanings. Body shape and posture affect how we think about ourselves. Finally, overall appearance relates to how the face, eyes, gestures, postures and shapes are perceived. Appearance is an inevitable part of the meaning derived from our body's movements. Another important type of non-verbal communication is proxemics - the study of how we communicate with space around us. Paralanguage is the closest to actual verbal communication. In paralanguage a different meaning is given to each statement. Though the same words are used, most communication is not verbal. Positive and negative messages may be sent through non-verbal communication - Manager's need to be effective communicators to achieve positive results in today's organisation. To be effective in choosing the right style of leadership to meet the needs of the situation, managers need to develop Analytical Skill, Flexibility Skill, Communication Skill and the Skill to communicate non-verbally.

4

Barriers to Communication

The communication must be interpreted and understood in the same manner as it was meant to be sent by the sender, otherwise it will not achieve the desired result and a communication breakdown will occur. There are certain external roadblocks to effective communication like noise, poor timing, incomplete, inadequate or unclear information, poor choice of channel of transmission of information etc., which can affect the proper reception of the communication. In addition, there are personal factors which may interpret the communication not in the same manner as it was intended by the sender but in a way that the receiver wants to receive, depending upon the stimuli present, emotions or prejudices for or against a concept or ideology or personal conflicts so that instead of interpreting the content of the communication, the intent of the sender may be interpreted.

The communication effectiveness is always influenced by our very natural tendency "to judge, to evaluate, to approve or disapprove the statement of the other person or other group." This evaluation tendency may alter the meaning of the entire communication. Accordingly, the management should not only attempt to eliminate all external barriers so that the communication is clear and to the point, but also try to understand the perceptions and attitudes of the receiver. Only then can the communication have its maximum effect.

Some of the organisational barriers and some of the interpersonal barriers to effective communication are discussed below:

4.1 Noise Barrier

Noise is any external factor, which interferes with the effectiveness of communication. The term is derived from noise or static effects in telephone conversations or radio wave transmission. It may cause interference in the process of communication by distraction or by blocking a part of the message or by diluting the strength of the communication. Some of the sources contributing towards noise factor are:

(a) *Poor timing:* One must know when to communicate. A message that requires action in the distant future may be forgotten by the time action is to be taken. Similarly, a last minute communication with a deadline may put too much pressure on the receiver and may result in resentment. A message must be sent at an appropriate time to avoid these problems.

(b) *Inappropriate channel:* Poor choice of channel of communication can also be contributory to the misunderstanding of the message. One must decide whether the communication would be most effective if it is written or by a telephone call or a face-to-face conversation or a combination of the modes. If the communication has been initiated through a telephone call, then it may be necessary to confirm the message of the call by putting it in writing. The face-to-face communication generally emphasises the strength of the message because it is supported by non-verbal gestures of eye contact, hand gestures, facial expressions, tone of voice etc.

If you want immediate action from the receiver, you would not send a lengthy discussion report, you would probably pick up the telephone or go to his office to tell him what to do. Remember also that one picture is worth a thousand words, and in this age of computer graphics the information can be produced more quickly in this way too.

(c) *Improper or inadequate information:* The information must be meaningful to the employee. It must be precise and to the point. Too little or too much information endangers effective communication. Ambiguity or use of words that can lend to different interpretations should be avoided.

(d) *Physical distractions:* One must recognise that in the case of face-to-face communication, any distractions can interfere with the process. Telephone interruptions, walk-in visitors or attending to other matters can interfere with the effective communication process. These external disturbances must be avoided.

(e) *Organisational structure:* The organisational structure should be such that the chain of command and channels of communication are clearly established and the responsibility and authority are clearly assigned. Communication may be blocked, chaotic or distorted if the channels are not clear and if the passages are blocked or if there are bottlenecks or dead ends.

(f) *Information overload:* As dynamic changes are continuously occurring in our life, in our society and in our organisations. Thus creating a mass of information to be processed. Overload occurs when individuals receive more information than they are capable of processing. The result could be confusion in processing of information or some important information may be laid aside for the purpose of convenience.

(g) *Network breakdown:* Network breakdown may be intentional or due to information overload and time pressure under which a communication has to be acted upon. Some factors contributing to such disruptions are:

- The managers may withhold important negative information.
- The secretary may forget to forward a memo.
- There may be professional jealousy resulting in closed channels etc.

Noise Barriers at Various Stages of Communication Process

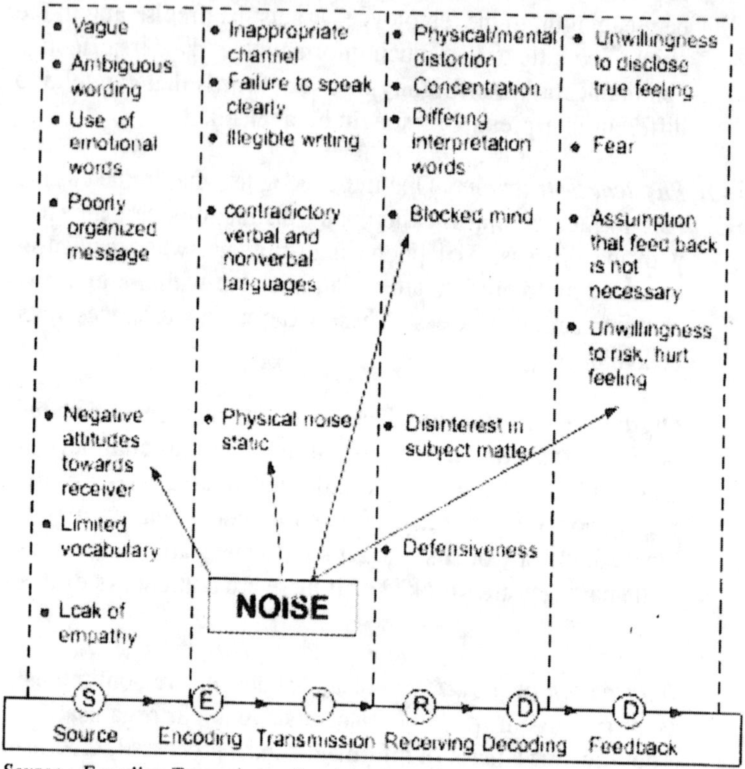

Source : Encoding Transmission Receiving Decoding Feedback.

Fig. 4.1.

4.2 Semantic Barriers

Occur when people use either the same word in different ways or different words in the same way. Do you know that there are 15 different meanings of word 'charges' in the English language? They also occur when people use terminology professional shorthand that expect others to understand, or language, which is outside the other's vocabulary.

These barriers occur due to differences in individual interpretations of words and symbols. The words and paragraphs must be interpreted with the same meaning as was intended. The choice of a wrong word or a comma at a wrong place in a sentence can some times alter the meaning of the intended message. Many times, we have to explain that "it was not what I meant" or "you misunderstood my message" etc. due to poor choice of words. For example, a nightclub advertisement sign, "clean and decent dancing every night except Sunday," could lead to two interpretations. First that there is no dancing on Sundays and second that there is dancing on Sundays but it is not clean and decent. Accordingly, it is advised that if there is any ground for misunderstanding in a message, that it be reconfirmed with the sender. For example, if you are giving your address to someone on the telephone, it is advisable that the receiver repeats this address so that the sender can verify it right away to reassure its effectiveness.

4.3 Feedback Barriers

Although one-way communication is quicker, two-way communication is more accurate. In complex situations, it helps both sender and receiver to measure their understanding and it improves their joint commitment to the task. It enables both parties to pick up and correct misunderstandings, leading to a higher quality of reception and acceptance.

Feedback is only to ascertain as to how the message was interpreted. Feedback closes the communications loop and is important for effective communication. It is equally important to pay attention to the feedback. The feedback may be for the purpose of communication; the results of an action or it may be for asking questions about the communication for further clarifications. A student who misunderstands a question in the exam, does not have the provision to ask for clarification and may end up giving the wrong answer.

4.4 Culture Barriers

Culture differences affect communication between people from different departments in the organisation. The culture differences can affect the communication effectiveness, especially for multinational companies and enterprises with multi-ethnic work force. Some examples are as follows:

- Advertisement about Action Man Soldier toys, where two soldiers were in tanks holding machine guns, were not permitted in West Germany where they were interpreted as promoting violence.

- In Australia and France, the children are not permitted to do television commercials.

- Most Jewish people will not work on Saturday and most Muslims will not work on Friday afternoons.

- Establishing deadlines to accomplish work assignment is considered rude in most Middle East Countries.

- Punctuality in some countries is not considered important.

- Many important meetings and actions are contemplated after consultations with astrologers in India.

- "Coke adds life" may be misinterpreted as a device for long life.

Accordingly, management must recognise these barriers as culturally oriented and identify these cultural differences and attempt to minimise any adverse effects on communication effectiveness due to these differences.

4.5 Barriers due to Perception

Having a poor self-concept or self-understanding or a poor understanding of others can cause perceptions. Perception relates to the process through which we receive and interpret information from our environment and create a meaningful word out of it. Different people may perceive the same situation differently. Hearing what we want to hear and ignoring information that conflicts with what we know can totally distort the intent or content of the message. Some of the perceptual situations that may distort a manager's assessment of people resulting in reduced effectiveness of the communication are:

- A manager may perceive people to belong to one category or another as stereotypes, rather than individuals. For example, he may perceive women to be less efficient managers or old people less hard working or lacking drive and creativity.

- A manager may make a total assessment of a person based on a single trait. A pleasant smile may give a positive first impression. Punctuality alone or loyalty alone may cause a favourable perception in the mind of the manager. This is known as the halo effect.

- A manager may assume that his subordinate's perception about things may be similar to his own. A manager, who accepts, added responsibility and challenges with enthusiasm may expect the same from his subordinates. This perception limits the manager's ability to effectively respond to and deal with individual differences and differing views of work situations.

The management must realise these differences in perceptions and take steps to understand the environment. A successful manager must be aware of the impact of factors that affect perception by interaction with others and should also possess the ability to influence the change of perceptions of others where necessary so that events and situations are interpreted as accurately and objectively as possible. For example, an employee may exist a message simply because the employee has not developed a trust in the manager due to past experiences. If the employee was promised a bonus or promotion on certain accomplishments and did not receive the promised rewards, he may tend to ignore the communication wherever possible. Accordingly, the manager must step-in to eliminate such negative perceptions among the employees.

Sender's Credibility

When the sender of the communication has high credibility in the eyes of the receiver, the message is taken much seriously and accepted at face value. If the receiver has confidence, trust and respect for the sender, then the decoding and the interpretation of the message will lead to a meaning that would be closer to the intended meaning of the sender. Conversely, if the sender is not trusted, then the receiver will scrutinise the message heavily and deliberately look for hidden meanings or tricks and may end up distorting the entire message.

Multi-meaning Words

• Many words in English language have different meanings when used in different situations. Accordingly, a manager must not assume that a particular word means the same thing to all people who use it. A study by Lydia Strong concluded that for the 500 most common words in English, there are 4,070 different dictionary definitions. For example, the word "run" can be used in 15 different, ways. Some of the examples are:

- I have a run in my stocking.
- Did you see him run?
- What headline do you want to run today?
- There was a run on the bank today.
- Who will run for President this year?
- Please run my bath water etc.

Accordingly, the managers must make sure that they use the word in the same manner as the receiver is expected to understand it, otherwise it will create a barrier to proper understanding of the message.

Language Differences

Language differences are often related to differences in individual perceptions. For a message to be properly communicated, the words used must mean the same thing to sender and receiver. The same symbolic meaning must be shared. Suppose that different departments of a company receive a memo stating that a new product is to be developed in "a short time". To people in research and development, "a short time" might mean two or three years. To people in finance department, on the other hand, "a short time" might be three to six months, whereas the sales department might think of "a short time" as a few weeks. Since many different meanings can be assigned to some words, great care must be taken to ensure that the receiver gets the message that sender intended.

Further barriers to communication may result from the use of jargon. People who have special interests or knowledge, such as software designers or behavioural psychologists, are often unaware that not everyone is familiar with their specialised terms. Sometimes people use jargon to exclude others or to create an impression of superiority — both of which make communication difficult.

Because words often have symbolic significance, using them as labels should be avoided. If we label certain people "show" or "unreliable," for example, we begin to see them that way. Worse still, such labels can become self-fulfilling prophecies. People so labeled may themselves begin to believe the labels and act accordingly.

Emotionality

Emotional reactions - anger, love, defensiveness, hate, jealously, fear, and embarrassment influence how we understand other's messages and how we influence others with our own messages. If, for example, we are in an atmosphere where we feel threatened with loss of power or prestige, we may lose the ability to guess the meanings of the messages we receive and will respond defensively or aggressively. The best approach is to learn to accept emotion as part of the communication process and attempt to understand them when they cause problems. If you are confronted with a subordinate behaving aggressively, try to sympathise. Get the person to talk his or her concerns, and pay careful attention to what is said. Once you understand the person's reactions, you may be able to improve the situation by modifying your own behaviour. In general, it is best to cultivate an atmosphere of rationality openness, and trust, encouraging subordinates to talk freely about themselves and their interests. Subordinates who are met with an emotional response whenever they have a problem or make a mistake may distort messages or avoid communicating altogether.

Inconsistent Verbal and Non-verbal Communication

We think of language as the primary medium of communication, but the messages we send and receive are strongly influenced by such non-verbal factors as body movements, clothing, and the distance we stand from the person we're talking to, our posture, gestures, facial expression, eye movements, and body contact. Even when our message is as simple as "Good morning," we can convey different intents by our non-verbal communication. A busy manager who does not want to be disturbed might respond to a subordinate's greeting without looking up from his or her work. A supervisor who usually frown will likely be unpopular with subordinates, despite his or her best attempts to treat employees kindly and fairly, if they react to his non-verbal cues rather than his verbal ones. The barriers to communication as described above are being represented in the following figure.

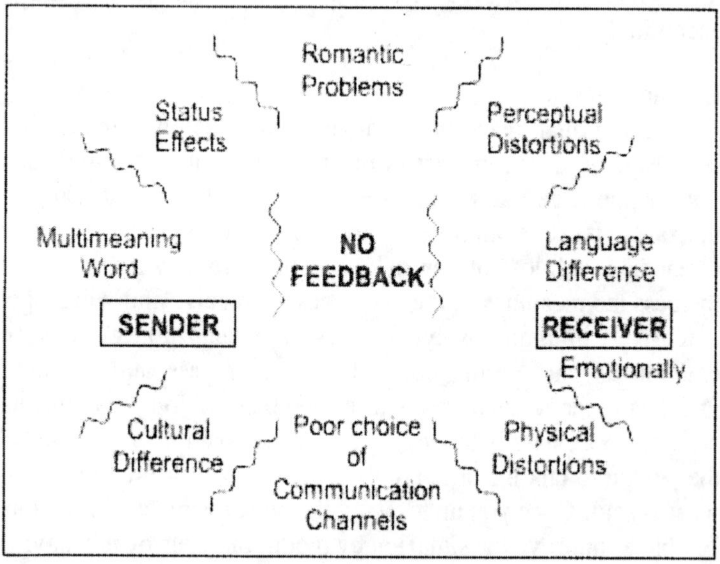

Fig. 4.2. Barriers to Communication

4.6 Summary

Communication must be interpreted and understood in the same manner as it was meant. Certain external roadblocks affect the proper perception of communication. These road blocks may be noise in the channel, semantic barriers, feedback barriers, cultural barriers, barriers due to perception, sender's credibility, multi-meaning words, language difference, emotionality, inconsistent verbal and non-verbal communication etc.

Noise is only external factor, which interferes with the effectiveness of communication. The strength of message may be diluted or some part of the message may be blocked due to any of the external factors like poor timings, inappropriate channel, improper and inadequate information, physical distraction, organisational structure, information over load, network breakdown etc. These may cause barriers at the source, encoding, decoding at feedback stage of the communication process. In addition there are some personal factors, which may not interpret the received message in the same manner. We should attempt to eliminate the external barriers, try to understand the perceptions and attitudes of receiver to make the communication more effective.

5

Overcoming Barriers to Communication

It is very important for the management to recognise and overcome barriers to effective communication for operational optimisation and this would involve diagnosing and analysing situations, designing proper message, selecting appropriate channels for communicating these messages, assisting receivers in decoding and interpreting and providing an efficient and effective feedback system. Some of the steps taken are as follows.

Overcoming barriers is a two-step process. First, one must learn to recognise the various types of barriers that can occur. Second, one must act to overcome the barriers. We describe below some of the techniques that can be used to overcome the specific barrier:

5.1 Overcoming Noise

Noise is best dealt with, by communicating it. If noise from a machine makes talking difficult, turn off the machine or move to a new location. If you notice that your receiver is not listening closely, try to regain his or her attention. Avoid distracting environments. Alternately, when noise is unavoidable, increase the clarity and strength of the message.

5.2 Feedback and Upward Communication

Feedback helps to reduce misunderstanding. The information is transferred more accurately when the receiver is given the opportunity to ask for clarifications and answers to any questions about the message. Two-way communication even though more time consuming, avoids distrust and leads to trust and openness that builds a healthy relationship contributing to communication effectiveness. Upward communication is strengthened by keeping an open door policy and providing opportunities for workers to give suggestions, which should be taken seriously by the management by acknowledging them and taking appropriate action.

5.3 Overcoming Different Perceptions

To overcome differing perceptions, the message should be explained so that those with different views and experience can understand it. Whenever possible, we should learn about the background of those with whom we will be communicating. Empathising and seeing the situation from the other person's point of view and delaying reactions until the relevant information is weighed helps to reduce ambiguous messages.

5.4 Overcoming Distrust

To overcome differing perceptions overcoming distrust is to a large extent the process of creating trust. Credibility is the result of a long-term process in which others recognise a person's honesty, fair-mindedness, and good intentions. There are few shortcuts to creating a trusting atmosphere; a good rapport with the people, one communicates with, can only be developed through consistent performance. Communication is a continuing process and the goal of the communication is complete understanding and trust. Accordingly, the management must be sincere and earn the trust of the subordinates. Management should not only be sensitive to the needs and the feelings of the workers, but also its promises should be supported by actions. The word of the management should be as good as a bond. Only then would an atmosphere of friendliness actuates, which would enhance the communication process. According to studies conducted by J. Luft, openness and an atmosphere of trust builds healthy relationship and closes any credibility gaps, thus contributing to communication effectiveness.

5.5 Overcoming Differences in Languages

To overcome language differences, the meanings of unconventional or technical terms should be explained. Simple, direct, natural language should be used. To ensure that all-important concepts have been understood, asking the receiver to confirm or restate the main points of the message is particularly helpful. In some cases, when all members of an organization or group are going to be dealing with a new terminology, it may be worthwhile to develop a training course of instruction to acquaint members with the new topic. Receivers can be encouraged to ask questions and to seek clarification of points that are unclear or may be misunderstood. It is also helpful to remain sensitive to the various alternatives interpretations possible for a message. Messages can often be restated in different terms. Sometimes even a minor change can have beneficial effects.

5.6 Overcoming Emotionality

The first step in overcoming the negative effects of emotionality is to increase one's awareness of them. Being sensitive to one's own moods and being aware of how they might influence others before communicating an important message to them is helpful. Trying to understand the emotional reactions of others and preparing oneself beforehand for dealing with emotional encounters are also useful approaches. On a more general level, steps can be taken to create an atmosphere in which destructive emotionality is unlikely. Fostering a supportive environment in which new or different approaches are given serious consideration reduces emotions. Employees should be given constructive feedback, if done properly, evaluations of employees, lead to improved trust and respect. The development of trust confidence, and openness results in a secure, non-threatening communication environment, and such an environment is less likely to produce emotionality and defensiveness.

5.7 Overcoming Inconsistent Verbal/Non-verbal Communication

The keys to eliminating inconsistencies in communication are being aware of them and not attempting to send false messages. Gestures, clothes, posture, facial expression, and other powerful non-verbal communications should agree with the message. Analysing the non-verbal communication of other people and applying what one learns to oneself and to one's dealings with others is helpful. Two additional approaches are generally useful in getting one's message across. The first is redundancy-repeating the message or restating it in a different form. Redundancy counteracts noise by reducing the uncertainty in the transmission of the message. The optimal level of redundancy varies with the circumstances. If a message is sent in a permanent form on paper, a tape or a disk, for example, then little redundancy within the communication is called for. On the other hand, if the message is extremely complex, it may be useful to repeat key points in several different forms even in a written communication. Redundancy is also more important in oral and other "perishable" forms of communication. If someone is giving us a phone number and we don't have a pencil and paper, we are more likely to remember it if it is repeated several times.

Like other techniques, redundancy can be overused. If we hear the same message too many times, we may become bored or angry. Eventually a receiver will come to treat such a message as noise. Furthermore, in some situations, storage of the redundant information can be a problem. Many libraries would like to have two copies of every book they buy, for example, but two copies cost twice as much, take up twice as much space, and take almost twice as long to-catalog. The money, space, and time might better be devoted to another book.

The second general approach is one that we have already mentioned, encouraging the development of an environment, or organisational culture, that supports giving and receiving feedback. Feedback is most useful when it focuses on things that the person who receives it has the power to change. Feedback on a spoken presentation, for example, can help the speaker improve his or her wording, delivery, and use of gestures: comments should emphasise these areas. The tone of the speaker's voice cannot be significantly changed, however, so there would be little point in commenting on this dimension of a performance.

Providing feedback helps both sender and receiver. In the telephone number example, the most useful action is to repeat the number back to the sender. This step not only helps in remembering it, but it also enables the sender to confirm the accuracy of the transmission.

Often, all that is necessary to obtain feedback is to ask if the listener understands what is meant. Non-verbal clues can also be useful in assessing a person's reaction. For example, one can give a speaker non-verbal encouragement by nodding one's head every few moments and maintaining direct eye contact. Managers to strengthen mutual respect can use the manner in which feedback is given.

5.8 Moving from Defensive to Supportive Communication

One important approach to overcoming communication barriers is described by Jack R. Gibb. Gibb has suggested that the type of behaviours or attitudes people manifest affects the way of the communication, while other types will cause people to feel they are supported-thereby facilitating communication. Defensiveness and supportiveness are briefly discussed in each of the six pairs of behaviours.

Evaluation description: If the speaker's manner, expression, tone, or choice of phrase is interpreted as a judgment about or an evaluation of the listener, then the listener may become defensive. This reaction is not unrealistic, since much communication is, in fact, evaluative. As managers, we will often find it difficult not to pass judgment on subordinates automatically. Conscious effort is sometimes needed to avoid this defense-provoking behaviour. Senders should pay careful attention to objectivity in communication. Receivers can test the quality of their understanding through the instructive suggestion of Carl Rogers: The next time you get into an argument... just stop the discussion for a moment and, for an experiment, institute this rule: "Each person can speak up for himself only after he has first restated the ideas and feelings of the previous speaker accurately and to that speaker's satisfaction".

Control-problem orientation: Statements, orders, or simple observations that seemingly attempt to control other persons imply that the speaker has better judgment and therefore that the listeners are inferior. Methods of communicating an attempt to control may range from a threat-backed command to a simple disapproving frown. Since these imply that the receiver is not capable of making a wise decision without direction, they create defensiveness even if the control is accepted. When the sender makes it clear, however, that he or she is trying to join with the receiver in defining and solving a problem, a supportive climate results and an improvement in communication is almost inevitable.

Strategy-spontaneity: If we think someone is "playing games" with us, rather than acting spontaneously, or usual reaction is resistance. Managers who have been superficially involved in sensitivity or human relations training frequently attempt to act spontaneously: the listener often senses an underlying insincerity. Genuine and honest communication, however, usually creates a genuine and honest response.

Neutrality-empathy: Communication that demonstrates empathy for the listener will produce highly favourable reactions. Conversely, a cold, clinical attitude will be seen as indifference and will lead to stiff, formal, less satisfying interchanges.

Superiority-equality: As we all know from experience, individuals who act superior do not usually get cooperative and friendly response. Those who lecture and give a warning will be received coldly. Those who talk as equals, on the other hand, and who indicate they trust and respect their listeners, will be usually received honest.

5.9 Improving Listening Skills

According to Stuart Chase, "Listening is the other half of talking" and is a very important part of the total communication process. Listening is an active mental process and goes beyond simply hearing. Good listening habits lead to better understanding and good relationships with each other. Some guidelines for effective listening are:

- Listening requires full attention to the speaker. Do not let your mind wander or be preoccupied with something else; otherwise you would not grasp the meaning of the message in its entirety.
- The language used, tone of voice, expression and emotions should receive proper attention, listen for feelings in the message content and respond positively to these feelings.

- Ask questions to clarify any point that you do not understand clearly and reflect back to the speaker your understanding of what has been said.
- Make sure that there are no outside interruptions and interferences during the course of conversation.
- Do not prejudge or value the importance of the message due to your previous dealings and experiences with the sender or your perceptions about him, positive or negative.
- Don't jump to conclusions before the message is over and is clearly understood.
- Summarise and restate the message after it is over to doubly make sure about the content and the intent of the message.

5.10 Developing Writing Skills

Clearly written message can help avoid semantic and perception barriers. A well-written communication eliminates the possibility of misunderstanding and misinterpretation. In writing messages, it is necessary to be precise, making the meaning as clear as possible so that it accomplishes the desired purpose. Rober DeGise suggests some helpful hints in written communications, as follows:

- *Keep words simple*. This will reduce your thoughts to essentials and will be easier to understand by the receiver. The message will be lost if the words are complex and do not lend to clear single meaning.
- *Do not be bogged down by rules of composition*. While the rules of grammar and composition must be respected, they should not take priority over the ultimate purpose of the communication.
- *Write concisely*. Use as few words as possible. Do not be brief at the cost of completeness, but express your thoughts, opinions and ideas in the fewest number of words.

- *Be specific*. Vagueness destroys accuracy, which leads to misunderstanding of the meaning or intent of the message. Accordingly be specific and to the point.

For overcoming the barriers to communication at sender, receiver and both ends, let us classify them at the following three groups and consider the actions that may be taken at each stage. These are:

- *Barriers to reception*: environmental stimuli the receiver's attitudes and values the receiver's needs and expectations.

- *Barriers to understanding*: language, semantic problems the ability of the receiver to listen and receive, specially messages which threaten his or her self-concept the length of the communication status effects.

- *Barriers to acceptance*: prejudices interpersonal conflicts between sender and receiver.

One way of reducing the effects of these barriers is to check continuously during the communication process as illustrated in Fig. 5.1. The actions we can take to achieve this are listed below:

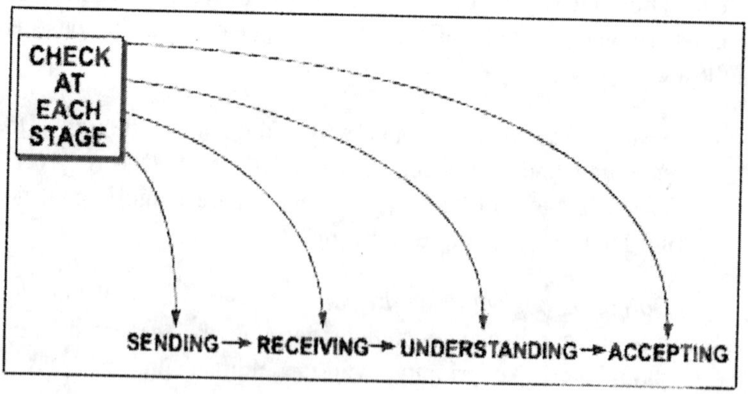

Fig. 5.1. Checking Communication

Sender:

WHO: to whom should the message go? Why am I communicating? What are my motives ?

WHAT: Decide what to communicate. Be clear about what you need to communicate.

WHEN: Choose the best time for optimum reception.

HOW: Use language the receiver will understand and which is unambiguous.

WHERE: Choose a location, which will not interfere with the reception, understanding and acceptance of the message: Privately? Home or away? In a group? At work or outside?

Keep checking with receiver.

Receiver:

Be fully ATTENTIVE to sender.

Listen ACTIVELY to the message being sent.

ASK for clarification, repetition where necessary.

Keep checking with sender.

Together:

Realise that misunderstandings are bound to occur, and be ALERT for all cues to this effect.

LISTEN, listen, listen and listen again.

TEST your understanding of the message.

Share OPINIONS, feelings and perceptions generated by message.

5.11 Summary

It is important to recognise and overcome barriers to effective communication. This is possible by diagnosing and analysing situation and then act to overcome this. By increasing clarity and strength of the message the noise barrier may be overcome. The healthy relationship between receiver and sender contributes to communication effectiveness. Avoid distrust and lead to trust and openness. The message should be so explained that even the people with differing views and experiences understand it. A person's honesty, fair mindedness and good intentions result into credibility and person is listened. Management should be sensitive to the needs and feelings of the worker's and should support by actions. Whether in verbal or non-verbal communications, simple direct and natural language should be used. Trying to understand the emotional reactions of others and preparing oneself before hand for dealing with emotional encounters are also useful approaches for overcoming barriers in communication due to emotionality. Non-verbal communication through face and eye, gestures, clothes, facial expressions etc. should be properly in tune with the message. In an organisation, encouraging the development of an environment or organisational culture is a good approach in getting one's message across. Whether people feel supported in such an environment, communication gets facilitated. Empathy for listeners produces highly favourable reactions. Most of the communication barriers may be overcome if, one has the improved listening skill: good listening habits lead to better understanding. Listening for feelings in the message content and responding positively to these feelings, improves communication effectiveness. Semantic and perception barriers may be overcome by clearly written message that requires skills in writing.

6

Developing Skills to Communicate Effectively

Managers, to be effective, need to develop communication skills, and any training or development programme should incorporate them. These skills can be learned on the job or on formal programmes, but require continual practice and reinforcement so that they become part of manager's toolbox when interacting with other people. They are:

1. *Listening*
2. *Giving and receiving feedback*
3. *Assertiveness.*
4. *Resolving conflict.*
5. *Solving problems.*

6.1 Listening

Actually, very rarely we listen; we receive only distorted or garbled messages. The information on which we make decisions is therefore of minor value for us, and affects our effectiveness. We need to learn to listen for all cues of verbal and non-verbal, which, interpreted accurately, will give us complete understanding of messages being sent.

6.1.1 Active Listening

Active listening requires definite commitment and personal discipline. You prepare yourself deliberately to concentrate and not to be influenced by external influences. It is time-consuming and you need to pay attention to the other person on three different levels.

As managers, it is critical to our effectiveness to listen to other people, but we all make conscious decisions on whether to listen, to half-listen, or to ignore communications from them. If the information confirms our current needs and beliefs, and if it helps us to satisfy our current needs, we are likely to listen intently. Information that conflict with either or both is likely to be rejected-try telling your boss that his department is not running efficiently!

We have to be careful not to discard important information as irrelevant noise. We make choices about listening: you may train a cat to listen to a melody on a piano. Introduce a mouse, and the cat shuts out the melody to concentrate on catching the mouse. People have the same ability. However, the more skilful we are at listening, the better we are likely to be at communicating generally.

Flow chart show below illustrates how we all communicate through our minds, our emotions and our body language. The mind selects the words, which convey the facts of the message. Our emotional commitment is shown in the feelings we express when delivering the message. We use body language to emphasise key facts and feeling.

MIND → WORDS → UNDERSTANDING

EMOTIONS → FEELINGS → MAKING CONTACT

BODY → ACTIONS → IMPACT

6.1.2 Active Listening Techniques

Active listening techniques help you communicate to others that you have heard and understood them. Implementing the following five active listening techniques can help your team communicate more effectively.

- Non-verbal listening responses
- Paraphrase
- Reflect the implications
- Invite contributions
- Reflect the underlying feelings.

Let's look at each of them in turn, examining examples of the techniques, their advantages, and tips for their use.

6.1.2.1 Non-verbal Listening Response

Used in conjunction with verbal active listening techniques, non-verbal responses increase your communication power. Beware, however, of using these non-verbal cues without really listening to what another person is saying. Such "fake listening" won't help you, and may even hurt you in the long run if another team member discovers that you weren't listening.

Examples	*Advantage*	*Tips for use*
Looking in to the speaker eyes	Communicates message and personal acceptance	Be sincere
Nodding approvingly		Be consistent
Leaning towards the speaker	Shows understanding and interest	Resist external distractions

6.1.2.2 Paraphrase

Paraphrasing is an active listening technique that helps you understand exactly what the other person is saying, and identifies

Examples	*Advantage*	*Tips for use*
"As I understand it....."	Shows that you are listening intently to the message	Listening intently
"What you're saying is....."	Clarifies the sender's "true" message	Paraphrase fairly often
"If I could summarize ......"	Helps you truly understand the message	May interrupt to do so

you as a careful listener. Use it regularly, and you'll avoid having to later clarify points you thought you understood at the time.

6.1.2.3 Reflect the Implications

When you reflect the implications of a message, you're going beyond merely understanding the words themselves. You're thinking ahead, reading between the lines, and showing that communication is a two-way channel.

Examples	*Advantage*	*Tips for use*
"Would that mean that....." "Are you saying....."	Communicates "genuine" interest in the message	Allow the speaker to be in control Avoid trying to persuade
"Would that help with......	Exhibits understanding of the message or issue being communicated	Avoid 'one-upmanship'

6.1.2.4 Invite Contributions

Inviting contributions, another active listening technique, allows you to show interest and to follow up on a good thought. It can encourage a shy speaker to continue explaining an idea, or communicate openness when you don't necessarily agree with the speaker.

Example	*Advantages*	*Tips for use*
"What happened then?" "Can you give me an example?" "Tell me more about	Communicates a desire to hear more about the topic. Allows time for the sender and receiver to understand the message. Promotes openness	Should not be used exclusively. Should follow paraphrasing and reflecting. Avoid "overexposing" the speaker.

6.1.3 Benefits of Active Listening

Active listening and feedback go hand in hand. They help to give and receive messages of greater clarity and understanding. Lets team members vent; gives them what they may want: an ear!

Lets team members feel appreciated, understood and accepted. Develops competence: 'enhances members' ability to identify problems and solutions; improves reasoning and judgment. Lets team members remain responsible and accountable; keeps the "money" on their backs and therefore lightens your workload. Avoids the "Yes, but........." trap. Allows members to think for themselves; builds independence. Saves time for all involved removes loaded or negative language by paraphrasing. Results in a better working relationship. Active listening benefits both speakers and listeners. If every member of your team uses active listening, you'll reap a durable reward!

6.1.4 Guiding Rules Effective Listening

- Be motivated.
- Make eye contact.
- Show interest.
- Avoid distracting actions.
- Empathy.
- Take in the whole picture.
- Ask questions.
- Paraphrase.
- Do not interrupt.
- Integrate what is being said.
- Do not over talk.
- Confront your biases.
- Make smooth transitions between speaker and listeners.
- Be natural.

6.2 Giving and Receiving Feedback

These skills, which we tend to overlook as we feel generally that we are pretty good in these areas. However, generally we are not! To establish and build on relationships we need to obey certain rules in our social interactions that will help us to improve. Most people find both giving and receiving feedback, handling praise and criticism equally difficult—the result is that we often only hear and listen when there is a real problem. Here are some hints for improving the provision of feedback:

1. *Comment on specific actions*: say "You sorted out that awkward problem very well" instead of "You are good with difficult problems". Equally, say "You didn't meet your sales targets this month" rather than "when are you ever going to meet your targets?"

2. *Give reasons for your comments*: 'pointing at the implications for not giving the discount, make it very clear why you couldn't do so'.

3. Concentrate on behaviour, which can be changed, which is within the control of the other person, rather than make personal comment about the individual.

4. Be descriptive, not evaluative.

5. Express opinions as opinions, not facts.

6. Be constructive, not destructive.

7. Avoid loaded terms, which produce emotional reaction/ defenses.

8. *Giving praise*: genuine praise is more likely to be accepted if it is for better-than-normal performance and if it is given straight to the performer, rather than beating about the bush.

9. *Giving criticism*: do not put down people in front of others when you have described the facts; seek solutions jointly with the other person in private.

10. Disagreeing with other:

- State your disagreement clearly: "No, I disagree with it".
- Be doubtful in a constructive way: "The difficulty I see is, how can we get round the constraints?"
- Be willing to change your opinion if more facts emerge. Give reasons for your disagreement.
- Recognise that others may have different points of view from yours.

Refusing requests:

- Keep your reply short and do not ramble-on justifying yourself.
- Give reasons if you want to, but do not invent excuses.
- Do not apologise profusely.
- Ask for more information if you need it.
- Ask for more time to decide if you need it.

Here are some hints on how to receive feedback:

- Listen carefully.
- Try not to let your hackles fise your defenses build.
- Note areas of question/disagreement.
- Paraphrase what you hear.
- Check your perception of what you hear.
- Ask for clarification/examples.
- Do not over-react to feedback.
- Evaluate its accuracy and potential value to you.

6.3 Assertiveness

How can you impress another person without necessarily upsetting him ? How can you be forceful yet sufficiently sensitive to the other's feelings? The answer is, by being assertive; each of us has our own personal space, both physical and psychological. "Full thirty inches from my nose the boundary of my person goes" wrote W.H. Auden and although the distance may differ from individual to individual, from culture to culture, the concept still applies.

The size of this personal space is influenced by our values, emotions, ideas and views about the world. People have a right to those values and do not thank others for encroaching on their personal territory. Assertiveness is a means of making an impact on other individual without encroaching on their personal arena; it is a means of influencing others without damaging your interpersonal relationships.

Assertiveness lies between submissive and aggressive behaviour (see Fig. 6.1). When you are submissive, you are unwilling or unable to express honest feelings, needs, values, and personal concerns. You let other people violate your personal space and crush your rights. When you are aggressive, you tend to walk on other people. You impose your points of view and values on them and express your feelings at the expense of theirs. You are likely to generate resistance in others by blocking their demands or views, and have difficulty in getting them to make commitments. Being assertive lets you say what you want, without overwhelming or abusing other people. You are clear about your own position and let other people know this, but can also accept that they may have other views and so may wish to negotiate their position accordingly.

Assertiveness training is a critical element in developing communication skills; it helps in all the following ways:

- Open, honest communication
- Learning to relax and reduce anxiety
- Getting more of your needs accepted

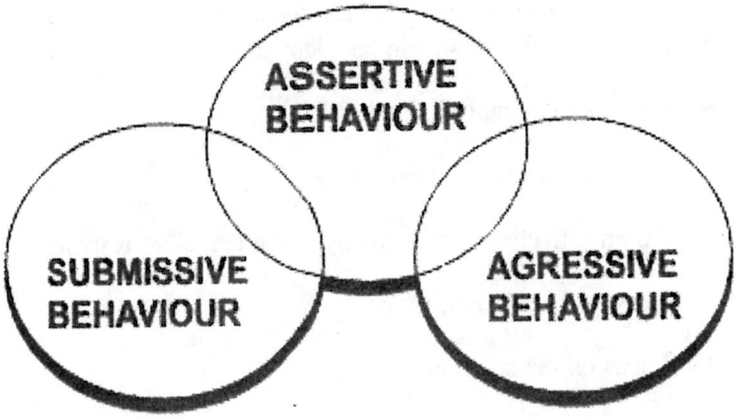

Fig. 6.1.

- Learning social skills that form closer interpersonal relationships.
- Taking responsibility for what happens in your life - at home, as well as at work.
- Making more decisions and free choices.
- Recognising that you have certain rights and your own personal value system.
- Protecting you from being taken advantage of by other people.
- Being asked to do something outside your job description.
- What changes do you need to make in your behaviour to be more assertive/less aggressive/less submissive?
- How can you achieve this?

Assertive behaviour is more likely to alter someone else's behaviour and less likely to violate his or her personal space; there is little risk of damaging existing relationships or reducing the other's self-esteem; and there is less likelihood to de-motivate, or risk uncontrolled defensive behaviour.

To improve the likelihood of success in an assertive approach, the following procedure should be adopted:

- Prepare thoroughly beforehand.
- Send your assertive message.
- Listen actively and reflectively to the defensive response.
- Recycle the process, if necessary.
- Focus on the solution.

Managers need to develop assertiveness skills to become effective communicators.

6.4 Resolving Conflict

Conflicts, tensions, problems with individuals or groups are inevitable in organisation. People are different: they have their own views or issues, their own approaches to solving problems. Interpersonal conflict arises just as much because of the manner in which discussions take place as from disagreement on specific issues. People can end up still disliking each other even after they have agreed on an issue simply because of the way in which the negotiations were constructed. The questions then are whether they will do what they have agreed. Are they committed to doing it? If not, this will eventually lead to further conflict.

To gain greater collaboration and commitment, you should consider these approaches in conflicting situations:

1. Use active and reflective listening:
    - to improve understanding of each other's positions and views of the situation/problem;
    - to generate trust so that you can be open and honest with each other.
2. Use assertiveness skills:
    - to make a powerful impact on others;

- to maintain their commitment to implement the agreed solution.

3. Reduce communication blockages between the parties:
   - do not try to dominate, to be aggressive, or to threaten;
   - do not make false judgments, e.g., confusing opinions with facts.

4. Concentrate on issues:
   - do not increase interpersonal tensions by criticism or negative feedback;
   - gather facts;
   - breakdown - large issues into smaller workable units then deal with each problem separately;
   - when you have reached agreement on one issue, consider how you can build on this to reach agreement on others.

5. Identify and appraise carefully the actions decided:
   - assess the consequences of these actions for both parties;
   - make sure you have a commitment for implementing the agreements; by whom, when and how?
   - identify areas of potential future conflict and try to agree joint approaches to them now.

6.5 Solving Problems

Solving problems is all about trying to find some form of mutual agreement about decisions and actions to be taken in problem situations. You, as manager, may have all the facts and resources at your disposal and may be therefore able to solve the problem without any discussion with other persons. This is not always the case! You may have to share with others the problem, the facts, the feelings in the situations, so that you can make a high quality decision. It may also be necessary to gain the total commitment of others to the decision so that it will be implemented successfully.

You will not necessarily achieve this if you make the decision by yourself. Two further communication skills are important for managers to improve their effectiveness: counseling and coaching.

6.6 Counseling

Despite the efforts to place people in well-designed, highly motivating jobs and to train them properly for those jobs, some people do behave in ways that cause problems for themselves and for the organisation. These problems may be work related, sometimes personal concerns and pressures which the individual brings to the job each day. Often a friendly suggestion or comment from the manager is all that is needed to remedy the problem. In more serious cases, the manager may have to counsel the employee to try to get him/her to change his/her behaviour or attitude. Situations requiring counseling can arise in different ways. Like:

- An employee may sense that he/she is not doing too well on the job, or may be having problems at home which are affecting his/her work, so he/she comes to the manager for help (this only occurs where there already exists a good boss-subordinate relationship).

- Employees may also come to their manager about problems they are having with other people. They want their manager to straighten out these other people. They may not see that they themselves are the problems. As far as they are concerned, they are OK (but those other people are not co-operating in the way they should.

- An employee's behaviour or performance is not up to par, or is causing problems with others; yet he/she is not aware of it. In this case the manager must initiate the action and bring the problem to the attention of the subordinate.

To develop skills in counseling, you need to follow a systematic approach and keep certain basic principles in mind. There are seven steps in effective counseling:

1. **Prepare for the Counseling Session**

    - think through what you want to discuss;

- give time for the employee to prepare;
- ensure privacy and no interruptions.

2. Define the Purpose of the Discussion

3. State the Problem

- state what the employee has done or not done (his/her performance), not the sort of person he/she is (his/her personality, his/her attitudes);
- try to find out and understand why the employee acted as he/she did (gaining insight), rather than evaluating his/her behaviour (passing judgment);
- make clear that your objective is to help the employee in future (develop him/her), rather than discipline him/her for the past (condemn him/her).

4. Get the Employee's Views

- has the employee described the situation as he/she sees it;
- used appropriate questioning techniques;
- restated/reflected what was said;
- listened to what is said, and what is left unsaid;
- do not jump to conclusions.

5. Clarify the Problems

- has the employee stated what he/she believes the problem really is;
- reach agreement so that he/she sees it as his/her own problem.

6. Help the Employee Develop a Solution

- ask for ideas;
- share information;
- agree specific courses of action.

7. Follow-up

- agree deadlines for actions;
- check that these deadlines are met;
- check that these actions are not causing further problems;
- keep on counseling as needed.

Counseling is a confidential, non-directive, face-to-face relationship. It is about helping people to understand themselves and the feelings particularly with regard to specific problems. Any problem which is presented to you is often just superficial, a symptom, not root cause. Your job is to help others to identify this before helping them to find their own ways of overcoming any difficulties they may face.

6.7 Coaching

You, as a manager, have a key role to play in the progress of your subordinates. One important way in which you do this is by coaching. You need to have a genuine desire to act as coach and help your subordinates to improve their effectiveness in their jobs. By doing so, they will perform better, and you have a better chance to meeting your targets. However, coaching takes time, and many managers feel such pressure for short-term results that they sacrifice long-term development on this altar.

The coaching process consists of three stages:

1. **Identify Opportunities for Setting Tasks which**

- have specific learning targets:

- are appropriate and relevant to the subordinate's job learning abilities and development needs within the organisation;
- can be measured and monitored.

2. **Set up Monitoring Systems**

- measure progress against deadlines, skill development;
- meet regularly to discuss and solve problems in a non-directive mode.

3. **Measure Task Achievement Against Targets**

- review performance when the task is complete;
- identify blockages and facilitating factors.
- jointly determine areas for future development.

Timing is critical for effective coaching. Do not try to coach when a subordinate is under extreme pressure of work—he or she must be motivated for effective progress to be made, and conditions and work situations must be favourable for successful coaching.

Communication skills required in coaching are:

- Setting clear targets which are attainable.
- Setting up and maintaining rapport in a close working relationship with the subordinate.
- Maintaining joint problem solving.
- Empathy for the feelings of the person being coached.
- Active listening.

Remember, learning is only effective when:

- the learner sees value

- it is active, not passive
- the timing is right
- it is built on experience
- it is consolidated with practice
- the learner can monitor progress
- it is geared to the learners capability and style.

If these conditions pertain, and you develop your communication skills, you can become an effective manager. The progress of your subordinates reduces the time you have to spend on direct supervision, and you will thus have more time to work on the other important elements of your job.

6.8 Summary

To communicate effectively, certain skills need to be developed You need to learn to listen for all cues of verbal and non-verbal which when interpreted accurately, gives the clear understanding of the message. Prepare yourself deliberately to concentrate and not to be influenced by external influences. One should not discard important information's as irrelevant noise. More skilful you are at listening, better you will be at communicating generally. Key facts and emotional commitment of your message are noticed by the words you use, your expression and actions.

Active listening technique viz. non-verbal listening responses, paraphrase, reflecting implications, inviting contribution and reflecting the underlying feeling help to communicate to others, that you have understood and heard them. While listening make eye contact, show interest, ask questions, paraphrase, be natural and make smooth transition to make speaker to feel heard and understood. One should avoid distracting actions and interruptions But being assertive you can be forceful, yet sufficiently sensitive to others feelings. Assertiveness is a critical element in developing communication skill. It helps in open, honest communication and learning social skills that form closer interpersonal relationships.

Managers need to develop assertiveness skills to become effective communicators. To gain greater collaboration and commitment of the people, managers should have the skills to resolve conflict and problem solving skills. If you develop your communication skills, you may become an effective coach and good counselor.

7

Ensuring Effective Communication

For ensuring better communication the accent should be on persuasion, it means that you transact your sessions with the communicatee in such a manner and spirit that he accepts - willingly and independently - what you had set out to suggest or recommend. The most important element of persuasive communication is good listening. Much of communication depends on listening empathetically not so much on talking. It deserves emphasis that: One communicates the most when one listens more than one talk.

7.1 Effective Listening

Graffiti on London bulletin board once had an excellent piece of wisdom. It read:

- Smart people speak from experience.
- Smarter people, from experience, do not speak.
- Rather: They (the smarter ones) listen.

It has been estimated by researchers that a typical manager spends about 80 per cent of his working hours communicating in one form or another. Out of this, about nine per cent of his time is spent in writing, 16 per cent in reading, 30 per cent in speaking, and 45 per cent in listening. Yet of all these skills, most people pay very little attention to building up their listening skills.

We have already enumerated poor listening as one of the serious barriers to communication. Let us see here what havoc it can play with the communicator and the communicatee if both are poor listeners.

In the case of a poor listening communicator:

- He can never get adequate information and feedback;
- Therefore, his communication, at best, can only be a shot at the dark; and
- In the end he either fails to put across what he wants, what does get across is distorted beyond recognition.
- He never gets to know or comprehend even simple message his own emotional or other filters distort the message;
- Interested parties can use him as an easy prey to motivated distortions; and
- Avoidable and unfortunate tensions, and misunderstand continue to dominate the scene.

7.2 Good Listening Practices

The prime responsibility for building up a good listening lies with the communicator. Good listening can be promoted in following manner:

1. *Take Care of your Body language*: Merely saying that you in 'open door' communication, and that anyone is free and was to come and tell you whatever he wishes to is not enough. He will feel like coming to you share information, thought and worries. This is locating manifested by the interest or indifference you show to on the course of your communication with them (through your responses or body language). You must acquire a convincing reputation that you do pay attention when someone comes to speak with you.
2. *Listen Perceptively*: Listening is not accomplished solely through what is being said. Try to concentrate on:

- How something is being said;
- What is not being said; and
- The body language of the speaker.

This habit of 'extra sensory' listening can open up to you a whole of information much vaster than what you can get from only the spoken words. Facts, while obviously important, are not the only thing to listen subjective data, such as thoughts, feelings, ideas, opinions and beliefs, also provide important information.

3. *When it is your turn to put across your message*: The stage you can do this if you:

    - Create a pleasant, business-like setting. A quite, comfortable office is one of the best places to establish a good communication environment;
    - Minimize interruptions. Limit telephone calls and visits by others so that your focus is on your communicatee; and pick a good time when both you and your communicatee are neither too tired nor overburdened with other worries or diversionary thoughts.

4. *Up your proposals when they are ripe*: Examine the following questions critically and candidly :

    - Is the proposal fully developed?
    - even if your people accept it, is it possible to act on it now?
    - Are your people prepared for acting on it now?
    - Even if the proposal is adopted now for action, will it conflict with other projects already under way?

For this you must remember the following:

- A desirable pre-requisite is that communication between you and your people should be an ongoing process - not one that you switch on only when a crisis appears or an important announcement has to be made. Such a practice creates an atmosphere of relaxed interactions; and relaxed interactions make it much easier for you to share even difficult messages with a greater degree of equanimity and acceptance;

- Take your time, especially when you are trying to get across new or complicated concepts;

- Unfold your ideas bit by bit; don't spring them on your people without a preamble or proper conditioning; and

- A good technique is to ask questions and invite questions and comments on the ideas or issues you wish to talk about. Provide freedom to them to speak frankly, and gently guide them to think and speak constructively.

5. *Don't make the issue bigger than it really is*: It may be that–

- In your anxiety to inject importance or enthusiasm among your communicatee's, you fall a prey to the temptation of painting a larger-than-life picture of the issue at hand. Be matter-of-fact; neither minimise nor exaggerate;

- The temptations to exaggerate - to stretch the benefits or minimise the problems - becomes strong when you have a particularly difficult proposition to get across. You must never do that Instead; you should frankly and realistically admit the difficulties and risks, as you perceive them. This may attract greater attention from the communicatee, and may even motivate them to try and meet the challenge;

- Messages about proposals or projects get exaggerated or distorted when passed from one group to another. Therefore, communicate personally, to the entire group of concerned individuals.

6. *Tell the whole story, you will find:*

    - It is far wiser, and more efficient, that you yourself give out the correct and adequate version, with proper emphasis of your choice. The full, and possibly the distorted, version is bound to come out eventually - thanks to the grapevine;

    - if you believe that some part of your message is likely to be unpopular, be sure to give that portion your meticulous attention, and to communicate that fully and honestly without any attempt to gloss over it or to lighten it. Such frank disclosure creates greater credibility for you, throws a challenge to your people, and may, possibly, secure their commitment to meet the challenge;

    - There is time to speak and a time to keep quiet. There are things to tell and things not to tell. But it is an excellent rule to practice frankness in all dealings and association with others, whether in business or socially. The frank person treads firm bridge crossing a river, while the secretive person charily steps from stone to stone.

7. *But do accentuate the 'positive'*: You are positive about what is most important is that;

    - You do firmly believe in what you are trying to convey to your people. Any lack of conviction on your part is bound to reveal itself to the searching eyes and ears of your people; and

    - Be sure to lay out the long-term benefits you are positive about, while you tell your people about the unpopular actions or results related with the proposal.

8. *Give the communicatee his say*: Especially when some 'heat' has been generated while you are communicating, you may feel like cutting of your communicatee in order to put across your own point of view. But a calmer and more persuasive approach is far more effective. You must:

- Keep yourself open accepting the communicatee's views and suggestions if they merit such attention; however
- You will do well to insist, in a gentle but firm manner, that the discussion must take place in a rational, unemotional spirit and tone.

9. *Itemize the message, and back-track*: If you watch carefully while communicating you will find that –

   - It helps the communicatee to comprehend and remember your message if you break it up in clear-cut items;
   - You can note whether your message is going across to your communicatee's by watching their expressions. You can thus adjust your style of speaking, and your body language. Accordingly, you should vary your style: the pitch of your voice, the sequence of the message, your body signals, etc.;
   - If you feel you are not getting across, or you have not got across fully, repeat your message in such ways that occur to you to be better. Try to anticipate objections, and 'cover' them in your communication before they are actually voiced. This saves you the both erection of 'rescuing' your message from batting, and goes a long way in making your message more acceptable.

10. *Project yourself into your listeners mind*: You must project yourself into the susceptibilities of your communicatee in order to understand his difficulties and hesitations, and to anticipate how he is going to react to your message. Whether you're trying to sell a product, please a customer, motivate an employee, or get along with someone, you will do better when you put yourself in the other person's shoes. To begin to do that, ask the following questions:

    - What experiences does the other person bring to this interaction?
    - What is the other person trying to achieve? What is the other person trying to avoid?

- Who else does the other person have to answer to? and

- What will it take the other person to consider the encounter with you a success?

- Don't fulfill people's wishes blindly, but do what you can.

11. *Be sensitive about timing*: Your communication of authentic facts must precede-not follow-the garbled versions thrown up by the grapevine. Once people get hold of the garbled versions. The task of clearing misconceptions and convincing people about the correct facts becomes stupendous sometimes a losing battle.

12. *Obtain nuances*: Getting factual reports are only one part of feedback. What is more important is to obtain the nuances, true and hidden meanings, feelings and beliefs behind the facts being reported.

13. *Feedback*: The single most important method for ensuring good communication is feedback. Communication without feedback is like a shot in the dark. When we seek feedback, we may, in many instances, be shocked at the kind of impact our so-called effective communication has made on the communicatee's. However, feedback cannot be had just for the asking. It requires creation of an environment based on mutual trust and freedom as perceived by the communicatee's for speaking out the truth to the communicator.

Feedback must be two-way from you to your people and from them to you. One most important precondition for promoting and sustaining two-way feedback is that you take the initiative of being frank and open. The more transparent your people perceive you to be in your intentions and statements, the more willingly they will open up to you. Authentic feedback sharpens your sensibilities - even while the communication session is in progress as to what and how to communicate. It opens your eyes to whether you have communicated at all; and if not, it tells you what you should do about it.

In other words, feedback helps us in modifying what and how we say things in terms of the 'real time' responses we get from our listeners. It leads us to greater accuracy, credibility and effectiveness in our communication. Feedback also automatically promotes multidirectional communication - upward, lateral and downward, thus fulfilling a very important pre-requisite of good communication.

14. *Interpersonal factors*: Climate, Trust and Credibility no matter how efficiently you use communication techniques, they will still not produce the desired results if the interpersonal elements are not conducive. These interpersonal elements comprise climate, trust and credibility.

Climate related to the relationship that exists between you and your subordinates who, in turn, depend upon how you treat each other, and how this reciprocal behaviour is interpreted. This combination of attitudes comprises the climate of interpersonal relationships; and it can promote, restrict or distort communication at the work place.

In the final analysis, communication is a give-and-take relationship between the communicator and the recipient; it is meant to produce a reciprocal effect on both parties. A major characteristic of all such relationships is trust. Distrust and suspicion between the parties can only lead to defensiveness, and inhibit open expressions. In such situations, even innocent and straightforward messages are looked upon with bias, and reactions to such messages are overloaded with counter-biases. The ultimate effect is that the chances of effective communication get nullified.

Closely related to trust, credibility refers to the perceived characteristics of the source of information. These characteristics may or may not be possessed by the source of information, but, what is important, they are attributed to that source by individual recipients of the message. In other words, the credibility of a source of information is recipient-determined.

The characteristics that are the essence of credibility are: honesty, competence, forward-looking attitude and inspiring leadership. When a communicator is perceived as trustworthy, knowing what he is talking about, dynamic and sincere, and having a sense of direction, others will see him as credible. And when he has credibility people are likely to comply with his requests, advice or instructions.

Credibility is one of the most vital ingredients of successful interpersonal communication. It can often cause insurmountable problems too. When you communicate, often your people do not listen to your words or read your message; they primarily assess your record of the actions and conduct to see the extent of gap, if any between what you preach and what you practice. Only if your people find that you can be trusted or if their perception of you is on the whole positive they will take note of your current communication, otherwise, not. Your current message, or the excellent communication techniques you may apply, nothing shall register in the mind of your people. In fact, the more you try, the more hostility and decision you are likely to evoke if you do not enjoy credibility in the eyes of your people.

15. *Express an interest in others*: Part of any communication strategy is showing an interest in others. People respond positively they can't help but respond when you show you are sincerely interested in them. Smile at them. Learn their names. Remember their birthdays. In fact, the more interest you take in others, the less bother - some you may find your own problems.

It is not only wise but also necessary that you take a sincere view of the interpersonal factors associated with you and your environment, and do something to bring these factors to an acceptable level if you wish to emerge as an effective communicator.

7.3 Guidelines for Improving Communicating Skills

Following guidelines are designed to improve skills in communicating so as not only to avoid any barriers to effective communication but also to strengthen the basis for optimum results which depends upon the clear understanding of the desired communication, these are:

1. *The ideas and messages should be clear, brief and precise*: The ideas to be communicated must be well planned and clearly identified. This will eliminate ambiguity so that the message will not be subject to more than one interpretation. The message must be clear, precise and to the point and free from distortions and noise. It should also be brief so that it is just necessary and sufficient and should avoid loose ends or meaningless and unnecessary words.

2. *Sense of timing*: The message should not only be timely so that the decisions and actions can be taken in time and when necessary, but also the timing of the message and the environmental setting in which the message is delivered and received is also very important. An important message delivered at the wrong time or in a non-conducive environment may lose its effectiveness. The environment involves physical setting, i.e. whether the communication is conveyed in private, and also it involves the social climate, which determines the work setting as well as interpersonal relationships.

3. *Integrity:* The communication must pass through the proper channels to reach the intended receiver. The communication flow and its spread must avoid by passing levels or people. When these concerned levels are omitted or by-passed, it created bickering, distrust, confusion and conflict. Accordingly, the established channels must be used as required.

4. *Consult with others who are involved in planning the communication:* If people have participated in the planning process, they would be highly motivated to give active support to such communication and carry it through. Also such participation would widen the scope and the objectivity of communication. The people who are concerned must know exactly what they need and when they need the communication. The purpose of the communication must be clearly known by all as to what is to be achieved and how.

5. *Be prepared to help the receiver:* Take the receiver's interests into account, then the receiver will be more responsive to

the communication. The management must clarify any part of the communication that may be necessary and must encourage comments, questions and feedback. The management must always be helpful in carrying out the intended message of the communication.

6. *Mode of delivery:* Not only the clarity on intent and the content of the message is important and necessary, but also the method of delivery. Avoid negative statements like, "I am not sure, it will work", but be confident and definitive. The success of the communication also depends upon the tone of voice, if the communication is verbal, expressions and emotions exhibited, attentiveness to the receiver etc. The written communication should be polite and unambiguous.

7. *Use proper follow-up:* Unless it is a one way communication, which is simply meant to inform, all communications need a follow up to ensure that it was properly understood and carried out. A verbal communication may need to be followed up by written confirmation. The response and feedback to the communication would determine whether the action to the communication has been prompt, appropriate and accurate. Inappropriate or delayed responses should be immediately investigated and corrective measures instituted.

8. *Communication should be comprehensive:* Communication should be complete so as not only to meet the demands of today but should also be based on future need of the organisation as well as individuals. A reasonable projection and assessment of future needs and environments both work and social should be incorporated, when planning and executing communication.

7.4 Tips for Good Communication

Following tips will help your team use the communication process to its advantage. Notice how differently effective and ineffective communicator respond.

Use these tactics daily. If you focus on a different one each day or week, you'll find your communication becoming more

Tips	*The Ineffective Communicator*	*The Effective Communicator*
Find areas of interest	Tunes out dry subject	Seeks opportunities; asks, "What's in it for me?"
Judge content not delivery	Tunes out of delivery is poor	Judges content; skips over delivery errors.
Hold your fire	Tends to interrupt or argue	Withholds judgment until comprehension is complete.
Work at listening	Shows no energy output; attention is "faked"	Work hard; exhibits active body state
Resist distractions	Distracted easily	Fights or avoids distractions; tolerates bad habits; knows how to concentrate
Exercise your mind	Resists difficult material; seeks light, recreational material	Uses heavier material as an exercise for the mind.
Keep your mind open	Reacts to emotional words	Interprets "colourful" words does not get hung up on them
Capitalise on the fact that thought is faster than speech	Tends to day dream with slow speakers	Mentally sums up; weighs evidence; challenges; listens "between the lines"

effective. The more you practice, the easier it becomes. The results improved team dynamics will speak for themselves.

One of the major problems in communicating with other people is that it occurs through different channels and at different levels. This is why so many communications become miscommunications. Personal beliefs, values and frames of reference influence the ways in which we send and receive messages. They cause us to communicate through four separate channels;

1. Facts (or what we perceive to be facts, based on our own experiences).

2. *Feelings*: our reactions on an emotional plane in a specific situation.

3. *Values*: fairly unchanging beliefs about us, our society are culture.

4. *Options*: attitudes we take about our own position in a given situation; views that are subjective, not objective.

We can use all these channels in any communication mode for ensuring better and effective communication.

7.5 Summary

To make others to receive and respond to your message willingly and independently, the power of persuasion is very strong. Good listening is an important element of persuasive communication. Poor listening is one of the serious barriers in communication. Poor listening cause for the unfortunate tension and misunderstanding dominates the scene. Good listening habits should be promoted, so that one will feel coming to you to speak and share opinion. You should create a pleasant situation free from overburdened with other worries and diversionary thoughts. Listening to others is the best way to learn, an active sport. Attentive listening encourages expression of views and sense of belongingness and togetherness. Speaker should be provided freedom to speak frankly and gently guide him think and speak constructively. There is a time to speak and a time to keep quiet.

While discussing certain issues, it should not be made bigger than what really it is and the communicatee should be given its say. When the time comes you must project yourself into communicatee's mind.

The single most important method for ensuring good communication is feedback. Feedback must be two-way from you to your communicatee and from communicatee to you. Without feedback, communication is like a shot in the dark. Feedback helps us in modifying what and how we say. We get real time responses from our listeners. It permits multidirectional communication. The interpersonal elements comprising climate, trust and credibility produce the desired result in interpersonal communication. Finally, communication is a give and take relationship between communicator and recipient. If you show an interest on others, others will show interest on you. If you listen others - others will listen you.

8

Experimental Learning Exercises

EXERCISE - 1

Objective : To demonstrate that people see things differently.

Procedure : Introduce the exercise by stating that often our eyes may deceive us. These examples of "optical art" shown in the following may be used.

Discussion Questions

1. In illustration A, is the box inside a room or are there two boxes?

2. In illustration B, are the lines pulled apart at the centre or are they parallel?

3. In illustration C, which end is out?

Key :

1. Yes, either end is correct

2. Parallel.

3. Either one.

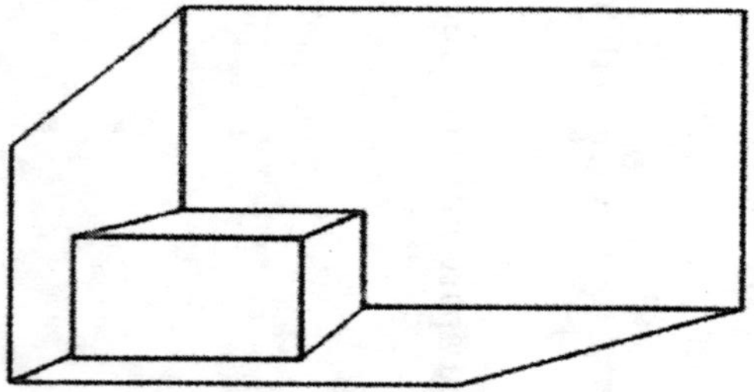

Fig. (A)

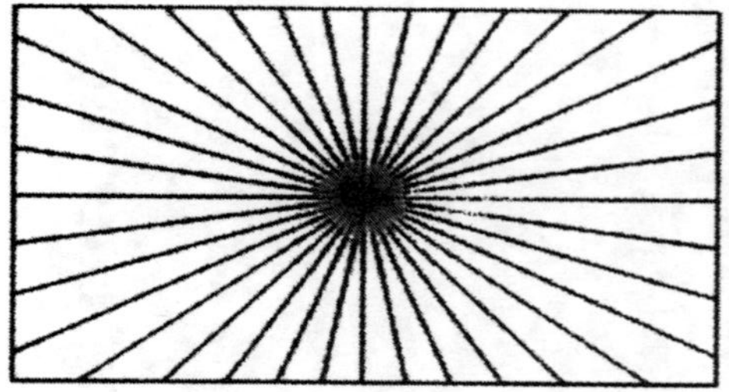

Fig. (B)

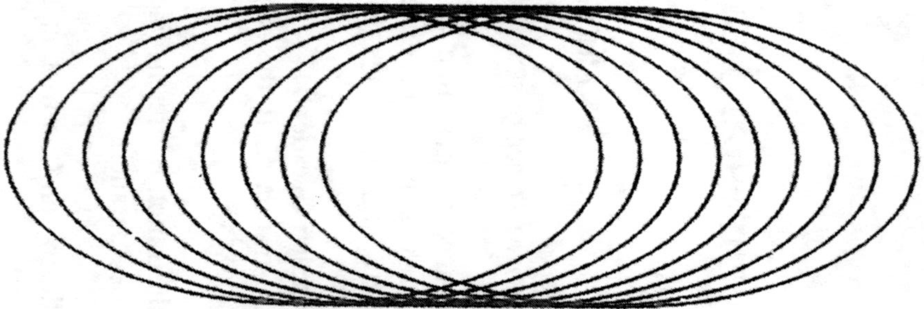

Fig. (C)

Discussion Question : 1. In Illustration A. is the box inside a room or are there two boxes?

Notes : Though the answer to these illustrations is simple as above yet, it is found that all the people in the group do not come to the same conclusion. This is due to the differing perceptions different people see things differently.

EXERCISE - 2

Objective: To demonstrate that "the eye sees, but the mind evaluates".

Procedure :

1. Exhibit the following diagram :

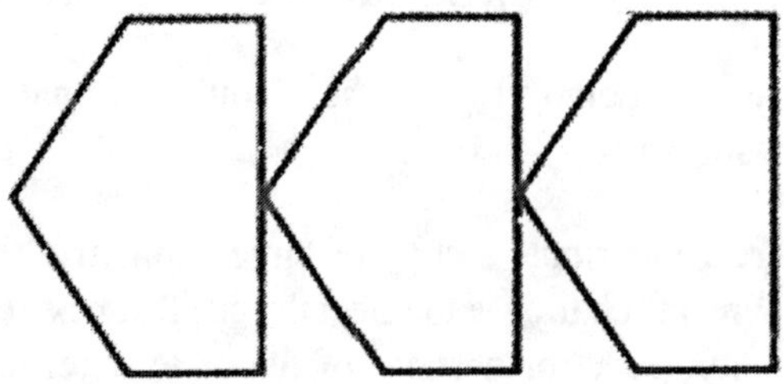

2. Ask the group "What do you see"? You may get responses like arrows, three triangles combined with three rectangles, three pentagons etc.

3. When you get the response "Two k's" immediately highlight the "two k's" and exhibit the next diagram.

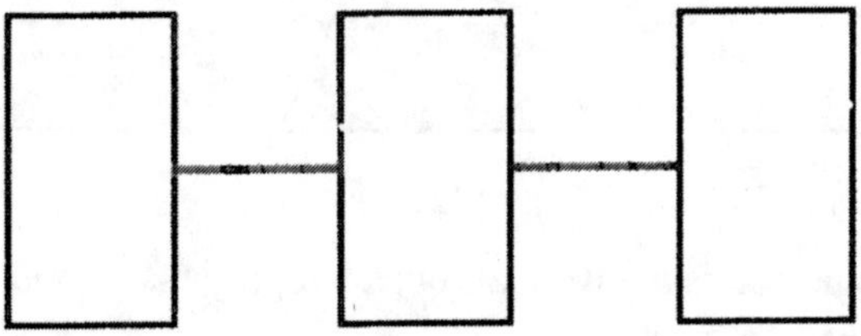

4. Then ask them "what do you see?" Very likely you will get the response "two H's".

Discussion Questions

1. Would you have seen the "H's" if some one had not first pointed out the "K"?

2. Why did you see the "H's" more easily than the "K's"?

3. In your work with people in what way is your eye seeing one thing and your mind another?

Notes : The reason for pointing out "K's" quickly is that now the context is known, people got conditioned :

- The eye saw and mind quickly evaluated.
- Responding to the familiar with context is easier.

EXERCISE - 3

Objective : To demonstrate the concept that "people differ in important ways".

Procedure : Distribute a copy of three geometric shapes as shown below: Direct each trainee to select the one that best represents his/her personality. Ask for a show of hands to determine how many selected 1, 2, 3. Then proceed (with great seriousness) to suggest that extensive research has shown the following characteristics to be associated with each shape.

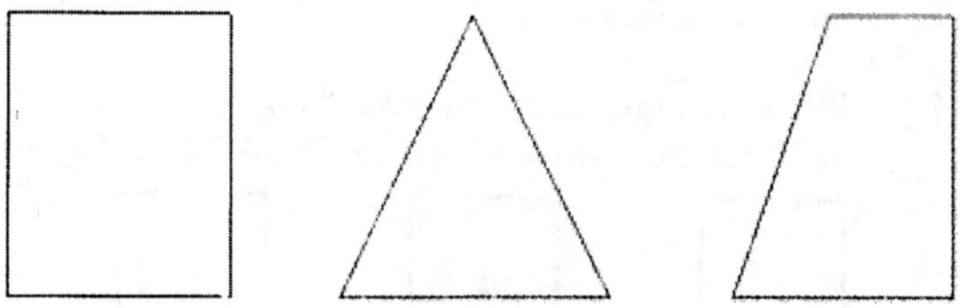

(1) (2) (3)

1. This person is intellectual, objective, rational, good decision maker.

2. This person is steady, dependable, and conservative and has perseverance.

3. This person is dissatisfied with the status quo, believes in no nonsense behaviour and tends to be a risk taker.

Discussion Questions

1. In what ways are people really different?

2. Is it possible to categorise people by such a test?

3. What are the dangers of stereotyping people?

Notes : Before the trainees are informed of the characteristics associated with each shape and after they have been informed, observe the ways how people differ and shift from one shape to another. Very interesting interpretations may come up from trainees for their initial and final choices of the shape.

EXERCISE - 4

Objective : To demonstrate that effective communication is a two-way process requiring both speaker and listener to be actively involved.

Procedure : Form pairs with trainees sitting facing each other. Trainees talk to each other simultaneously about "Everything I did since getting up this morning". Each trainee is to concentrate on one's story and should keep talking all the time. Continue for one minute.

Discussion Questions

1. What was happening between the two speakers?

2. Were they communicating?

3. Why? Why not?

4. How could communication improve?

Notes : It becomes noisy when trainees sitting facing each other talk simultaneously. Nobody is listening. The very objective of communication is lost. Information's are only sent but not received. Talking each other down improves the process of communication.

EXERCISE – 5

Objective : To demonstrate that one-way communication is limited.

Procedure : Let A and B form a group. A has a drawing sheet, and B is given a sheet of plain paper. A and B sit back to back. A now describes the drawing and B produces an identical copy on his sheet of paper. During the process B is not allowed to ask any question. When complete, compare the drawings.

Discussion Questions

1. Should B feel difficult to draw, why?

2. How did the listener 'B' feel? (frustrated, confused, angry).

3. Are there variations in finished/original drawin if yes, why?

4. What does this say about communication?

5. How could communication be more effective?

Notes : When the listeners are not allowed to ask questions as it happens in one-way communication, then the intended message received at the receiver's end is not the same as the message intended by the sender. Variations in finished and original drawing are an example of how one-way communication is limited.

EXERCISE – 6

Objective : To demonstrate that the two-way communication improves effectiveness.

Procedure : Let A and B form a group. A has a drawing sheet, and B is given a sheet of plain paper. A and B sit back to back. A now describes the drawing and B produces an identical copy on his sheet of paper. During the process B is allowed to ask questions, Where he feels confused. When complete, compare the drawings.

Discussion Questions

1. Should 'B' feel difficult to draw: why?

2. How did 'B' feel when confusions cleared?

3. Are there the variations in finished and original drawing? If yes, to what extent?

4. What does this say about communication?

5. Was communication effective?

Note : When 'B' was allowed to ask questions, it resulted in greater accuracy between finished and original drawing. It illustrates the importance of effective listening and checking out what was being said.

EXERCISE – 7

Objective : To demonstrate how words, when not coupled with face-to-face contact, are susceptible to incorrect assumptions and interpretations.

Procedure : Place two chairs back-to-back and select two people to sit on the chairs. Ask one to describe to the other a humorous or silly thing that happened to him. The incident could be recent or sometimes ago. As the one person speaks, the other person is asked to listen intently who in turn will report back.

Discussion Questions

1. As observer, did you tend to see and hear the same message? why?

2. As speakers or listeners, how did it feel knowing your words and actions were being closely monitored?

3. In real life situations how do you handle this?

4. How can we ensure more effective communication in cases like this?

Note : The message sent could not be correctly understood and interpreted if there is no face-to-face contact between speaker and listener. During verbal communication, non-verbal expressions like eye contact, gestures, postures and nodding head play vital role in sending/receiving the message.

EXERCISE - 8

Objective : To demonstrate that there is a significant danger to even simple instructions being misinterpreted by the receiver especially if:

1. Ambiguous words are used.

2. The receiver does not ask for clarification.

Procedure : Give each participant a sheet of paper and these two rules (Each one must close his eyes and not ask any questions during the exercise):

1. Tell them to fold their paper in two halves and then to tear off the bottom. Right corner of the paper.

2. Tell them to fold their paper in half again and then to tear off the upper right hand corner.

3. Tell them to fold the paper in half again and then to tear off the lower left hand corner.

4. Instruct them to open their eyes and display the unfolded paper to each other.

Discussion Questions

1. What words in the directions could be interpreted in different ways?

2. How could the directions have been better stated so as to reduce the ambiguity involved?

3. How can we encourage the employees to raise questions for clarification when they don't understand?

Note : There is a great possibility, that there will not be the same shapes of sheets of paper for want of clarification and clarity in instructions, rather uses of ambiguous words.

EXERCISE - 9

Objective : To demonstrate trainees become aware of body language and the extent of its use in every day communication.

Procedure : Form groups of 5 to 6. Give each group a set of emotions. A volunteer selects emotions and then tries to communicate the emotions non-verbally to other members. The other members have to guess the emotions.

Discussion Questions

1. Were we correct in our expressions and interpretations of emotions?
2. How much do we communicate in non-verbal ways?
3. Is it a language we can learn to use as we do with spoken language?

Note : When we communicate we use not only our voices but also our bodies. 70-80 per cent of our communication with others is non-verbal, i.e., facial expressions, body posture, gestures, tone of voices, mannerism etc.

EXERCISE - 10

Objective : To demonstrate the importance of some of our non-verbal behaviour.

Procedure : A pair of trainees sit back-to-back and begin a conversation about "The man I like". Continues for one minute. Pair next sit facing each other and carry out a conversation "The TV. Serial I like". Continues for one minute. Pairs sit facing each other and carry out a conversation but sitting on there hands about "The clothes I like to wear". Continues for one minute. Pairs pretend to be both deaf and dumb. They are to plan a summer holiday together but can only communicate by mime.

Discussion Questions

1. How did you feel when you have no eye contact, could not use hands and could not speak?

2. How important are eye contact, gestures and facial expressions to communications?

3. Are non-verbal ways of communication so important?

Note : Our own non-verbal behaviours, we should know. When we were restricted in use of our non-verbal behaviour, our awareness was sharpened for the use of these behaviours.

EXERCISE – 11

Objective: To demonstrate the Non-verbal listening behaviour.

Procedure : Let A and B form a pair. B begins a conversation on "How I feel about my organization". A responds non-verbally. Allow 1-2 minute for conversation. B guesses and tries to interpret about A's non-verbal responses, and evaluates variety of listening and non-listening situations.

Discussion Questions

1. How do you feel when you are not listened to?

2. How do you feel when you are listened to?

3. How 'B' might have felt in non-listening situations?

4. How 'B' might have felt in listening situations?

5. What happens when people do not listen each other, what happens when people do listen to each other?

6. Which is more important talking or listening?

Note : The strategy focuses on body language and looks specifically at listening behaviour. Listening is a critical part of the communication process. It is to be considered an active rather than passive activity. It is a skill that is complex and one, which improves with practice. We show we are interested, attentive and listening through posture, voice, eye contact, facial expressions, gestures, spatial distance, head movements etc.

EXERCISE - 12

Objective : To draw attention to the behaviours that block communication.

Procedure : Demonstrate variety of non-listening behaviour e.g., Yawning, looking at watch, fidgeting, no eye contact, bored expressions, body tuned away from speaker. Let A and B form a pair: 'A' talks 'B' "if I had been the Prime Minister of India" 'B' uses a variety of non-listening behaviour that continues for 1-2 minute and swap role.

Discussion Questions

1. How did it feel when they were not listening to?
2. How did it feel when they were listening to?
3. What happens to a relationship when people do not listen?
4. Do you experience the blocking of communication?

Note : Not only the non-listening behaviour blocks the communication but many of us inject communication blocks into our conversation by advises, interpretations and judgments. Putting down and talking "me, me ...." also block the communication.

EXERCISE - 13

Objective : To demonstrate the effect of careful listening and following the directions.

Procedure : Ask the participants to place a clean sheet of paper in front of them. Ask them to spell out two words from these letters using all of them: OODRTSWW.

Key : The letters and directions spell "TWO WORDS".

Discussion Questions : What did this teach you about the need to listen carefully?

Note : In the procedure itself the clue for the key word was given which comes out only after careful listening and following the directions accurately.

EXERCISE - 14

Objective : To demonstrate that listening can be improved when ones interest is induced.

Procedure : Read an article (three-four paragraphs) from a journal or magazine in which most participants can identify with i.e., their organisation, city, opportunities or some other area of interest. Ask them to write down as much as they can remember about the story.

Discussion Questions : Upon hearing something most of us forget 50 per cent just that fast. Why then, in the sample above, did many of us score so well?

Note : Doing so well is the result of effective communication between the sender and receiver as the receivers received the message understood, remembered and responded well.

EXERCISE - 15

Objective : To develop skills of empathy in communication by active and effective listening.

Procedure : Select a topic of controversial nature from a magazine or local newspaper. Select a Speaker, Listener and Referee. The speaker who, without interruption, explains his feelings on that topic discusses the selected topic. After the Speaker has finished, the Listener summarises (without notes), what was said on the subject following this segment. Speaker and Referee can correct or amplify any item stated by the listener. After 8-10 minutes, select a new topic and reverse role, using the same procedure. After another 8-10 minutes, new topic and role reversals are used, thus each person acts in each of three roles.

Discussion Questions

1. In your role as Speaker, did you sense any difficulties or experience any awkward moments?

2. How about as Listener or Referee?

3. Did you identify or observe any barriers that obstructed effective listening?

4. In your role as Listener, why was it difficult to summarise and paraphrase the Speaker's Comment?

Note : Communication that demonstrates empathy for the listener will produce highly favourable reactions. Conversely, a cold clinical attitude will be seen as indifference and will lead to stiff formal, less satisfying interchange.

EXERCISE - 16

Objective : To demonstrate the effect of careful reading and following instructions.

Procedure : You are supplied with a sheet, read carefully and follow the instructions.

SHEET:

NAME__________________DATE________________________

1. Read all the instructions before carrying out any action.

2. Put your name and date in the upper right hand corner.

3. Draw five small circles in the upper left hand corner.

4. Put a smaller circle in 3rd circle.

5. Put an arrow going out from 3rd circle.

6. Make the length of arrow 5 cms.

7. On the reverse of the sheet write IIIII.

8. Sign your name on the sheet.

9. Write "I have read carefully and followed instructions on the sheet".

10. Now that you have finished reading this carefully, carry out the instructions given in sentences (1) and (2). Do not carry out any of the other instructions.

Key : Name KRRIM, Date 29.3.2013.

EXERCISE – 17

Objective : To explain and exemplify the difficulty of listening.

Procedure : A conversation is taped with different bits of information's. After participants listen to the tape, ask 6-8 questions on items included in the message. Then play another recording and ask participants to listen intently. Again ask 6-8 questions.

Discussion Question

1. What barriers to effective listening did this exercise illustrate?

2. How can we motivate others to listen more attentively?

Note : Experience indicates most people can correctly answer only half of the questions of the message just listened. May be it is due to lack of interest or attention, emotions distractions etc.

Bibliography

1. Communicating for Managerial Effectiveness, *Philip. G. Clampit.*

2. The Essence of Effective Communication, *Ludlow R. and Panton F.*

3. Organizational Behaviour, *Kolb D.A., Rubbin IM and McIntyre J.A.*

4. Managing More Effectively, *Varma M.K.*

5. Success Through Team Work, *Chang R.Y.*

6. Effective Small Group Communication, *Ernest G. Borman, Nancy C.Borman.*

7. Management Theory and Practice, *J.S. Chandan.*

8. Conversation as Communication, *Gerard M. Blair.*

9. Business Communication, *Raymond V. Lesikar and John D. Pettit Jr.*

10. Presentation Skills, *ISTE Publication-Institutional Development Series.*

11. Written Communication Skill, *ISTE Publication - Institutional Development Series.*

12. Communication in Organisation, *Layman W. Porter and Karlene H. Roberts.*

13. Managerial Psychology, *Harold J. Leavitt.*

14. Organizational Behaviour, *Hellerigeel D.J., W. Slocum. R. W. Woodman.*

15. Work and Motivation, *V.H. Vroom.*

16. Some Management Skills, *A. Das Gupta.*

17. The Practice of Management, *Peter F. Drucker.*

18. Providing the Two-way Communication, Hand Book of Business Administration, *Becker, Esther R.*

19. A Few Thoughts on Communication, State Bank of India, monthly review Jan. 70, *A.K. Mazundar.*

20. Ten Commandments of Good Communication, American Management Association, 1955.

21. Effective Communication on the Job, American Management Association, 1956.

22. Of Human Interactions, *Luft. J.*

23. Barrier and Gateway to Communication, *Rogers, Cart R. and F.J. Roethlisberge.*

24. Management, *James A.F. Storier and Charles Wankles.*

25. Organization Behavior, *Stephen P. Robins.*

26. Management of Organizational Behaviour, *Paul Hersey and Ken Blanchard.*

27. More Games Trainers Play, *Edward E. Seannell and John W. New Storm.*

28. Module-Interpersonal Communication, PDU.

29. The Power of Persuasion, *Rupert Eaiers White.*

30. Body Talk, *Desmond Morris.*

31. Using language, Cambridge, *Clark H.H.*

32. The evolution of communication, *Hanser M.V.*

33. Social physiological models of interpersonal communication, *Kranas R.M. and Fussel S.R.*

34. Speaking from intention to articulation, *MIT Press*.

35. Spatial perspective – taking in conversation, *Schober M.F.*

36. Internet sources.

37. Social and non-social speeches, *Scientific American*.

Index

W